PRACTICAL PARENTING TIPS

PRACTICAL PARENTING TIPS

OVER 1500 HELPFUL
HINTS FOR THE FIRST FIVE YEARS

VICKI LANSKY

BARNES & NOBLE BOOKS

NEW YORK

Published by MJF Books
Fine Communications
322 Eighth Avenue
New York, NY 10001

Practical Parenting Tips
LC Control Number 2004104113
ISBN 1-56731-672-7

Manufactured in the United States of America on acid-free paper ∞

MJF Books and the MJF colophon are trademarks of Fine Creative Media, Inc.

QM   10 9   8   7   6   5   4   3   2   1

Contents

Dedication

To my granddaughter Sienna,
the first of my first and a joy to behold.

Introduction

My first child had the good grace to arrive at the end of May, so I was able to wheel him to the park almost daily. For him there was fresh air and sunshine—for me there were other new mothers on the park bench. It didn't take me long to discover that their babies also changed their waking schedules frequently, had leaky diapers, and were fussy in the evenings when we adults longed for private time. To my relief, I found I didn't have the only child who hadn't read Dr. Spock and responded as the book implied! Not only did I get support from those other mothers, I got a lot of ideas from them. Other mothers, I soon found, were a wonderful source of information.

In my first book, *Feed Me I'm Yours*, I simply wanted to share the baby food ideas that worked for me and other mothers. My subsequent books followed in the same vein: the desire to share what really works for parents. This book is a collection of the best childcare tips to help make the first five years with your children easier and lots more fun.

I now have the joy of being a grandmother and watching my son take care of his child. I continue to learn by watching. He and his wife find easy ways to keep life on an even keel. They're even open to listening to some of my suggestions.

People often ask me what my favorite tip is. Usually it's the last one I heard that was new for me and made me say, "But of course, why didn't I think of that?" This book is packed full of great ideas, so it's important to remember the most important tip of all:

There is no way you can do every tip in this book. Trying them all could lead to a nervous breakdown or, at the very least, an intense case of guilt.

—*Vicki Lansky*

PRACTICAL
PARENTING TIPS

Chapter 1

New Baby Care

Having a baby is like entering a long tunnel. You can't see the end and you wonder what you've gotten yourself into. You emerge five years later having had less sleep than you might have wished, but thinking it wasn't that rough after all. The difficult days become difficult to remember.

Despite the newness of caring for your first baby, it won't take you long to become an old hand at baby care. Babies don't arrive with attached instructions, but they do express their needs loud and clear. Luckily, they don't realize that everything you do is just as new for you as it is for them. Whew!

Don't worry if you don't feel overwhelming love for your infant immediately. It often takes time, perhaps months, for real parental love to develop. Relax and enjoy the developing bond between you and your baby.

Spreading the News

- Take advantage of your computer by sending e-mail announcements and digital photographs, or by printing announcements and sending them through the regular mail.

- Use a fabric marker to write your baby's name, birth date, weight, and length on the front of a single-color outfit or onesie.

Photograph your baby wearing the outfit, and send copies as birth announcements.

- Imprint your baby's foot several times on paper cards using a nontoxic ink pad. The cards will make lovely announcements or thank-you notes.

Your New Baby and You

Amid the flurry that follows the birth of a baby, it's important to remember that everyone has adjustments to make. If it's your first child, you'll have new roles to try out. If you have other children, their positions in the family will be changed overnight, too.

Along with the excitement and pride come stress and fatigue. You're apt to demand a great deal of yourself, which can take its toll on those around you. Take care of your personal needs so you can help others take care of theirs. Be especially good to your partner during this time, and put off any big decisions, if possible.

Adjusting to Your New Life

- Buy or make a "Do Not Disturb" sign, and hang it on your front door whenever necessary. Or create a personalized sign such as "Ssssh! Baby and Mommy Are Resting!"

- Turn the telephone ringer off when you don't want to hear it, or disconnect the phone if it doesn't have a ringer switch.

- To avoid answering the phone when you don't want to, record the details of your baby's birth on your telephone answering machine or voice messaging service. You may wish to add the best time to call. (You should be sleeping when your baby is.)

- Put an extension phone in your baby's room, or carry a cord-less phone with you when you need to change a diaper.

- Make an effort to create "parents only" time each day (a late dinner after your baby goes to bed, a walk around the block while a friend or relative watches your baby, a five-minute telephone call during the day, and so on).

- Use paper plates and cups to minimize housework, or have your helpers do the dishes. This is not the time to prove you can do it all and that nothing has changed.

- Get support from friends and relatives who've had babies, or become involved in community parent groups.

Cesarean Deliveries

If you're pregnant and planning to have a C-section, make some important decisions before going to the hospital. Talk to your doctor about the timing of the surgery (before or after your labor begins), the people who will be present during your delivery (the baby's father or anyone else), anesthesia and pain medication, your baby's care after the birth, your anticipated hospital stay, and any services available to you after the delivery.

If you're planning to breastfeed, make sure the doctors and nurses are informed ahead of time. Many childbirth education classes offer additional information on planned C-sections.

When You Get Home

- Stay in bed as much as you can. Keep your baby in a bassinet or crib near your bed, and keep a good supply of diapers and baby clothes nearby.

- Get a robe that buttons all the way down the front. It'll be easier to get in to and out of than one that opens only part way down.

- Wear comfortable, protective underwear to keep loose clothing from rubbing against your incision, unless loose clothing alone is not irritating.

- After bathing, gently dab the tender area with a soft towel, or use a hair dryer.

- Protect your incision while nursing by putting a regular pillow or a C-shaped pillow in your lap, or by putting your arm underneath your baby and holding her head at your breast.

- Try making a playpen of your bed if you must care for a toddler, too. Keep plenty of toys and books within reach.

Caring for Tender Abdominal Muscles

- Avoid bending down when dressing or changing your baby. Use an elevated changing table instead of a bed or other lower surface.

- Avoid holding your baby in one arm while doing things around the house, until your muscles are stronger. If your baby is fussy and wants attention, consider a mechanical baby swing.

- Use your foot as a lever to raise your toddler off the floor when you're in a chair or bed, instead of leaning down to pick your child up.

- Don't vacuum for a couple of months. The movements involved are hard on abdominal muscles. (It's a good job for a father, partner, or other family member.)

- Many mothers claim that rocking in a chair an hour or more each day relieves abdominal discomfort and intestinal gas.

Feeding Your Baby

One of the reasons why babies spend so much time eating is their stomachs are only the size of their fists. Consuming a lot of milk at one time just isn't possible.

If you're breastfeeding, the first rule is to relax. Find a quiet place away from distractions, and don't watch the clock. Your baby doesn't.

If Dad or your partner feels left out, there are plenty of things to be done, such as changing diapers, bathing your baby, and bringing your baby to you for feedings. Some parents decide to give their baby one bottle of formula or expressed breast milk a day, to let Mom get some needed sleep or a chance to get out of the house. If you use powdered infant formula, it's easy to mix up one bottle at a time.

Support for the Nursing Mother

La Leche League International provides information and support for breastfeeding women. For information on a group in your area, visit their website at www.lalecheleague.org; call 800–LA–LECHE (Monday through Friday between 8 A.M. and 5 P.M., Central Standard Time); or write to them at 1400 N. Meacham Rd, Schaumburg, IL 60173.

Dressing Comfortably for Breastfeeding

- Use a front-buttoning nightgown or one with concealed slits. Bring one with you to the hospital.

- Wear a stretch bra that can be lifted up for nursing. Some women buy nursing bras before they go to the hospital, getting a size larger (and a cup size larger) than what they wore during pregnancy, but this doesn't work for every woman. Consider buying a bra extender in a sewing notions department for the extra "give" you may need.

- To prevent leaks from soaking through your bra cups, use soft handkerchiefs, three or four layers cut from an old undershirt, two-to-three-inch circles of terry cloth stitched together, or a sanitary napkin or diaper cut to fit. Half a panty liner may be all you need. Nursing pads and other commercial products are also available.

- Wear printed tops to make stains less visible if you leak.

- If you're concerned about modesty, unbutton your blouse from the bottom, or wear a cotton T-shirt or pullover that's easily lifted up. Your baby's head will cover your bare midriff, and the T-shirt will cover your breast.

- Keep a cardigan sweater, scarf, or receiving blanket handy for a quick coverup.

Comfort Setups for Nursing

- Protect linens and blankets while nursing in bed by covering them with a crib-size waterproof pad.

- Use a big pillow with arms, or a C-shaped nursing pillow, for breastfeeding in bed. Some nursing pillows have Velcro straps that fasten around the mother's back.

- When nursing your baby on chilly nights, wrap up in a big blanket or get into a snuggle sack together. Or have a sweater or robe available. Your milk will flow better if you're warm and cozy.

- Select a cushioned rocker, armchair, or sofa for nursing while sitting up. Choose one with low arms to rest your arms on, and put a pillow under your nursing arm for added support. If you're thinking about buying a rocker, remember that a wooden one will be easier to clean than an upholstered one, though perhaps not as comfortable.

- Place a thermos with a warm drink, or a sports bottle filled with a cool drink, near the area where you'll be feeding your baby, so you can have the drink you need. Keep a few energy bars there, too.

Nursing Techniques

- Keep track of which breast you started on last time by transferring a safety pin from one bra strap to the other. Or move a lightweight expandable bracelet or fabric hair "scrunchie" from one wrist to the other. Some women use a ring that's loose enough to transfer from hand to hand.

- Keep your baby awake and sucking by gently rubbing her cheek.

- When you want to stop nursing, put your finger in the corner of your baby's mouth to break the suction and ease the infant off your breast.

- If your baby falls asleep while nursing, change her diaper to wake her up when you're ready to change breasts.

- Wear a bright necklace with colored beads or ribbons for your baby to look at and play with while nursing.

- Some babies find it hard to settle down against slippery nylon or polyester. If you're wearing a shirt of either fabric, slip a diaper or receiving blanket between you and your baby.

- If you're engorged and your baby isn't ready to nurse, express some milk in a warm shower or bath, or place a warm compress on your breasts before expressing milk.

- Experiment with various breast pumps, if possible, to find the one that works best for you.

- Stop an older baby who bites while nursing by pinching your baby's earlobe just hard enough to be a distraction.

Bottle-Feeding

A baby's food needn't be warm, but it goes against the grain for some parents to serve up a cold bottle. A fancy electric bottle warmer isn't necessary, though. Take the chill off in one of the ways suggested below. Test the temperature of the milk by squirting a drop or two on your wrist; if it feels comfortably warm, then it's okay for your baby. While it isn't critical for development, some parents hold their baby in one arm for one bottle-feeding and the other for the next, to help the infant develop good eye-muscle coordination.

- Warm a bottle by standing it in a couple of inches of hot water in a bowl, pan, mug, or other container. Or run hot tap water over the bottle. Shake it occasionally to warm the contents evenly.

- Be extremely cautious when warming a bottle of formula in a microwave. Formula heats unevenly and can scald your baby's mouth. Make sure to shake it *very* well before testing it on your wrist. If it's too warm, add more cold formula, then shake it and test it again. Avoid heating expressed breastmilk in a microwave, since it may reduce anti-infective properties.

- Cool an over-warm bottle by adding some cold milk or formula from the refrigerator.

- Thaw a bottle of frozen breastmilk by letting it stand at room temperature until thawed, by running it under lukewarm water and gently turning (not shaking) the bottle, or by letting it sit in a pan of warm water. Never thaw it in a microwave, as this may reduce anti-infective properties.

- Freeze expressed breastmilk in small amounts (two to four ounces) in clean glass or hard plastic bottles. Allow some room for expansion during freezing. Mark the storage date and use before six months. Thawed breastmilk should be consumed within forty-eight hours.

- Freeze expressed breastmilk in an ice cube tray. (Each cube is about one ounce.) Store the cubes in a plastic bag, and mark the storage date. Defrost the cubes in a liquid measuring cup and pour into a bottle.

- If you're traveling and need to keep formula or breastmilk cold, put reusable, self-filled, plastic frozen ice balls in the bottles. They won't dilute the formula or breastmilk. Or keep the bottles in a small cooler.

- If you want to take the chill out of a bottle when eating out, ask for a glass half-filled with hot water and place the bottle in the glass for a minute or more.

For an Even Flow

- Regulate the flow of formula by loosening the bottle collar if the flow is too slow, or tightening it if the flow is too fast.

- Enlarge nipple holes, if necessary, by inserting toothpicks and boiling the nipples for three minutes, or by sticking a very hot needle into the nipple a few times. If the hole is too big, toss the nipple and start using the extras you bought.

- To prevent powdered formula from lumping, put the powder in first, then add water. Cap the bottle or pinch the nipple shut, and shake vigorously. Or use a wire whisk and warm water to help dissolve formula more easily.

- Eliminate air from bottles with disposable liners by pressing up on the liner until the liquid reaches the tip of the nipple. This allows your baby to drink in an upright position. (Use leftover liners to cover recipe-type index cards!)

- Have your older baby use bottle straws inserted into traditional nipples. Formula will flow evenly no matter what position the bottle is in.

The Business of Bottles

- Keep bottles together and prevent tipping by storing them in an empty six-pack container in the refrigerator. Or make a large batch of formula and store it in a sterilized glass coffee pot in the refrigerator.

- Seal a can of baby formula with a plastic pet-food lid before refrigerating. Powdered formula comes in premeasured, single-serving packets.

- Use the lids from Heinz strained baby juices on Evenflo baby bottles.

- Label your baby's daycare bottles by writing your baby's name on masking tape and attaching it to a wide rubber band wrapped around the bottle. It's easy to remove and there's no tape to clean off the bottle. Or write your baby's name on the bottle with an indelible marker.

- Prevent bottle leaks while traveling by placing a plastic sandwich bag or a piece of plastic wrap over the top of the bottle before screwing on the nipple and collar ring.

- If your baby doesn't like holding a cold bottle filled with juice or milk, slip a sock over the bottle to keep little hands warm.

Cleaning Bottles

- Use your vegetable steamer basket to help clean or sterilize nipples, rings, and bottles. Open the steamer and turn it over to keep all the pieces under its umbrella in a pot of boiling water. While sterilizing bottles is no longer considered necessary, some parents like to use this procedure the first time they use the bottles or when their children are sick.

- Don't be afraid to wash bottles in the dishwasher; they don't need to be sterilized. To run nipples, caps, and bottle rings through the dishwasher, place them in a zip-up mesh bag like the ones used to wash pantyhose, or use a plastic basket designed for this purpose.

- Clean nipples and glass bottles by boiling them in water in a glass jar in the microwave. A teaspoonful of vinegar in the water will prevent hard water deposits in the jar.

- Use denture cleaner tablets to clean glass baby bottles. Let the bottles soak for half an hour according to directions. Swish with a bottle brush and rinse.

- Rinse out empty bottles as soon as possible, or you'll find "cottage cheese" in them later. If you don't have a bottle brush, put warm water and some dry rice in the bottle, and shake to scrub out milk rings. To get rid of a sour-milk smell, fill the bottles with warm water, add a teaspoon of baking soda, shake well, and let stand overnight.

- Remove juice stains by putting baking soda and warm water in the bottle and scrubbing with a bottle brush. If you don't have a bottle brush, use a pastry brush or something similar.

- Clean bottles by putting a dab of toothpaste on your bottle brush and just enough water to scrub them clean.

- Wash dirty bottles before going to bed at night, and fill them with the proper amount of water so they'll be ready for nighttime or next-day mixing.

Burping

Don't worry if your baby doesn't always burp after a feeding, especially if you're breastfeeding. If your baby seems comfortable after you've given it a good try, forget it. Be careful not to pat too hard, since you may cause your baby to vomit. Some parents find it better to use a gentle upward stroke instead of patting.

- Put your baby on your shoulder with a diaper or burp cloth underneath, and gently pat your baby's back between the shoulder blades.

- Tie a bib around your neck if you get tired of a burp cloth, and switch the bib from shoulder to shoulder as you switch your baby.

- Lay your baby on your lap, tummy down, with your baby's head turned a little to the side. Pat or gently rub from the bottom up.

- Make a "horseshoe" with your thumb and index finger, and hold your baby's chin while she's propped on your lap leaning against your arm. Pat your baby's back (or stroke upward) with the opposite hand.

- For an older baby who has good head-and-neck control, put your hand under your baby's sternum, lean your baby toward your palm that's draped with a burp cloth, and firmly but gently rub your baby's back with the opposite hand.

- Place your baby upright against your shoulder in your lap. Squeeze your baby's back gently, beginning at the kidney area and working slowly up to the shoulders.

Putting Your Baby to Sleep

Some babies sleep for long stretches, others take catnaps, and some prefer sleeping during the day rather than at night. Most sleep after being fed. A new baby who sleeps through the night (considered six hours straight) is the exception, not the rule, whatever your friends and relatives might say.

Sometimes babies need a little time to cry or fuss before sleeping. You'll soon know if the crying means something serious. Your first thought will be for your baby's comfort. During the first three to six months, parents usually have to adjust their sleeping habits or do baby care in shifts to avoid exhaustion.

The American Academy of Pediatrics recommends putting your baby to sleep on her back, since research has shown that this reduces the risk of SIDS (Sudden Infant Death Syndrome). Never put your baby to sleep on her stomach unless your doctor instructs you to do so. You can use a specially designed side-sleeping cushion to prevent your baby from rolling onto her stomach. Put your baby to sleep on a firm mattress, and remove all pillows, bumpers, quilts, and other soft items from your baby's crib.

It's neither necessary nor practical to create a silent sleeping environment for your baby. If you maintain a reasonable level of noise, your baby will become accustomed to it. You may wish to play soft music or white noise just outside your baby's room. If the telephone ringer wakes your baby, turn down the volume or turn it off completely. Or put a thick potholder under the phone to muffle the sound.

Waterbed Warning!

Never put your infant to sleep or leave your baby unattended on a waterbed, sheepskin rug, sofa, or other soft surface. Infants or children with disabilities can suffocate in the facedown position or by getting caught between the waterbed mattress and frame.

Inducing Sleep

- Try to establish a sleep routine as a sleep pattern emerges, especially if you'll be traveling or having your baby sleep in different places. Sing the same lullaby, give your baby a massage, bathe your baby, read a familiar story, nurse or give your baby a bottle, and so on. Establish an order of events and try to stick with it.

- Let your baby sleep upright occasionally, especially if he's congested. Place him in an infant seat or car seat or carry him in a front pack.

- Place a warm heating pad or hot water bottle on the crib sheet when you pick your baby up for a feeding, so the bed will be warm when you put your baby back down. (Remove the pad or water bottle first, of course.) Or warm a blanket in the dryer while feeding your baby, if that's convenient. A cold bed may startle your baby.

- Tape-record the sound of a running dishwasher, shower, or water filling the tub; play the tape while lulling your baby to sleep. The soothing sound of running water simulates the sounds from the womb. Or invest in an electronic toy or teddy bear that simulates intrauterine sounds.

- Read to your baby while rocking him to sleep. The sound of your voice may quiet your baby.

- Put your baby down while drowsy to help him learn to fall asleep without your help.

When Your Baby Confuses Day and Night

Confusing day and night is often associated with colic. If you or your partner is home with your baby during the day, you should catch up on your sleep by napping when your baby naps. If you're both working during the day, alternate baby shifts at night so you can both get some sleep. Try to encourage longer periods of wakefulness in the early evening by keeping your baby slightly cool and upright in an infant seat. Talk, sing, dance, read, or do whatever will stimulate your baby.

- Add a little instant cereal to the bedtime bottle to make a heartier meal. While not scientifically substantiated, this helps some babies sleep longer at night. Talk to your doctor first.

- Relax your baby by bathing her before bedtime.

- Dim the lights for the last feeding so your baby will realize it's time to go to bed. Consider using the crib only at night. During the day, put your baby to sleep in the playpen or infant seat.

- Consider waking your baby for daytime visitors, unless your baby gets extremely crabby when a nap is interrupted.

Making Night-Checking Easier

You wouldn't be the first parent of a sleeping baby to put a small mirror under your child's nose to check for breathing, but it's best to avoid this tension-producing habit.

- Install a dimmer switch on the light in your baby's room.

- Use a nightlight or two.

- Use an electric Christmas candle or decorative mini lights. They give off just enough light to see by.

- Keep a flashlight near your bed.

- Consider putting a lit aquarium in your baby's room.

- To prevent crib side rails from squeaking at night when raised or lowered, spray them with nonstick vegetable oil, apply some petroleum jelly, or rub them with waxed paper.

Keeping Your Baby Cozy

- Test for comfort by gently touching the back of your baby's neck. (Make sure your hand is warm; hold it next to your body or under hot water first, if necessary.) If the neck is warm, your baby is comfortable. If it's damp, your baby may be too warm. Arms and legs can also give a hint as to your baby's comfort; you can check for a pink or rosy color. (Very rosy may indicate heat and/or a fever.) Don't go by the feeling of your baby's hands and feet. They usually feel cool.

- Use blanket sleepers of various weights, depending on the season, and skip a blanket altogether. If you're really worried about your baby being cold, put on two blanket sleepers, but make sure they don't cut off circulation.

- Use a rubberized flannel lap pad to cover the crib sheet, or spread a diaper across the sheet to avoid having to disturb your baby after every leak and spit-up. (Rubberized flannel is available in large pieces in many fabric stores.)

- Cover the bassinet pad with a standard pillowcase. Flip the pad over for a fresh side when needed.

- Make your baby's bed with two or three layers of sheets and waterproof pads. If your baby leaks or spits up during the night, simply remove the top sheet and pad.

- Position your baby in a corner of the crib or bassinet to provide an additional sense of security. This also allows you to move your baby from corner to corner if the bed sheet gets wet.

When Your Baby Cries

Babies cry and fuss for a variety of reasons. Try to learn your baby's different cries as early as possible, so you can identify the solution quickly. Obvious solutions are available for common problems such as hunger, pain, fatigue, discomfort from being too cool or too warm, boredom, overstimulation, and needing to be held. When parents hear the loud, shrill cry of a baby in pain, they often check for a pricking diaper pin or a tiny thread tangled around a baby's hand or foot. Experienced parents check clothes and bedding first and clip all such threads.

Sometimes a baby cries...and cries...and cries...and nothing seems to help. Don't take it personally. Your baby isn't crying because you're a bad parent.

Coping with Crying

- Walk or dance with your baby. Try different kinds of music to see what works.

- Rock your baby in your arms or in a rocking chair.

- Take your baby for a ride in the stroller.

- Bounce your baby gently in your arms, on a bed, or in a bouncy seat.

- Take your baby for a ride in the car. (Always place your baby in a government-approved car seat. Make sure the car seat is properly installed and your baby is properly buckled in. Never place your baby in the front seat. The safest place is the middle of the back seat.

- Put your baby in a mechanical baby swing. Support your baby's head, if necessary, with rolled receiving blankets, towels, or a specially designed infant pillow.

- Run the vacuum cleaner, clothes dryer, fan, or a hair dryer.

- Offer your baby a noise-making toy such as a rattle or shaker.

- Sing or talk to your baby in a quiet, singsong way.

- Carry your baby in a front pack, close to your body.

- Lay your baby tummy-down across your lap, and gently rub his back. Make sure your baby's airways aren't obstructed. You might want to sway your knees slowly back and forth.

- Lay your baby across a warm hot-water bottle on your lap or on a bed. Test the bottle's temperature by placing it against your forearm.

- Use the football hold by carrying your baby facedown on your forearm with your baby's face supported by the palm of your hand.

- Gently massage your baby's torso and limbs using warmed lotion or baby oil. A semidark room may also help.

- Swaddle your infant in receiving blankets.

- Feed and burp your baby one more time, or offer a little warm water.

- Offer a pacifier. Molded pacifiers allow less air to pass in and are better for colicky babies. Hold it gently in your baby's mouth, if necessary.

- Let your baby suck the underside of your finger. (The pinkie usually fits best.) Turn your nail down so it doesn't poke the roof of your baby's mouth.

- Breathe slowly and calmly while holding your baby close. Your baby may sense your calmness and quiet down. Or place your baby near your heart while holding him close.

- Fold your baby's arms across his chest, and hold him down firmly but gently on the crib mattress, as if swaddled.

- If *nothing* works, have someone else take over for a while, or put your baby in the crib, close the door, and turn on the TV or radio. Take a shower to relax and drown out the noise. Check your baby every ten minutes or so.

Colic

Colic is not a disease. It can't be tested for. It's characterized by inconsolable crying that lasts one to several hours at a time, usually in the evening between six and midnight. Doctors don't know what causes colic, but it often reflects an unusual sensitivity to stimulation or, in breastfed babies, a sensitivity to certain foods.

In addition to crying intensely, colicky babies may pull up their legs, clench their fists, pass gas, and flush bright red. Fortunately, colic rarely lasts beyond the third month. Breast-feeding mothers may consider eliminating dairy products, spicy foods, onions, garlic, and caffeine from their diets. If you're using formula, you may consider switching to a different formula, but talk to your doctor first.

- Try burping your baby before a feeding to prevent a bubble from becoming trapped at the bottom of the stomach. Also, try burping your baby during a feeding.

- Use plastic bottle liners for bottle-feeding. Squeeze the air completely out of the bag before starting, to prevent air bubbles from causing abdominal discomfort.

- Place your baby in an upright position while feeding to allow air bubbles to escape more easily.

- Lay your baby in the crib face-up, and gently pull her left arm and right leg away from her body. Repeat with the right arm and left leg. This may help relieve gas.

- Check your local health food store for a homeopathic remedy called Gripe Water, a mild tonic that can't hurt—and may help.

- Steep a heaping teaspoon of dried chamomile flowers (available in health food stores) in one cup of hot water for five to ten minutes. Cool to room temperature, and give your baby two tablespoons three or four times a day.

- Let your baby suck on a peppermint candy stick, or melt a small piece of peppermint in water and give it in a bottle. Peppermint often has a soothing effect.

- Attach a SleepTight device to your baby's crib. It simulates the sound and vibration of a car riding down the highway. Information is available at 800–NOCOLIC or at www.sleeptight.com.

Keeping Your Baby Clean

You won't be giving your baby a tub bath until the umbilical cord falls off (and the circumcision heals). Babies don't get particularly dirty in the early months except for their bottoms, faces, and necks. A day without a bath isn't a disgrace. In fact, until babies start to crawl, they need to be bathed only two or three times a week and shampooed once or twice a week. First babies probably get bathed more often simply because parents have more time.

If you and your baby feel the need to relax together, a long, warm bath may be just the right thing. You'll soon learn which time of day works best for bathing. Some parents prefer to give baths shortly after feeding, even though it may increase the risk of baby spitting up.

Bath Equipment

- In the early weeks, you can make do with a plastic dishpan. You really don't need more than a few inches of warm water. Line the dishpan with a small towel to prevent slipping.

- Bathe your newborn in an inflatable baby tub, or use a sculptured foam liner in a larger plastic tub.

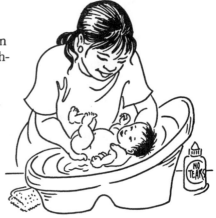

- Bathe your baby in the bathroom or kitchen sink. Make sure the faucet is moved out of the way or padded in some way.

- Use a hand-held shower hose or kitchen sink sprayer. Your baby will enjoy the running water, and you can rinse his whole body easily. Spray gently to avoid stinging his skin.

- Wear cotton gloves or socks on your hands to improve your grip when holding and washing your baby. Or make bath mittens from old towels.

- Tie or pin a large bath towel around your neck, like a bib, to keep you dry and to provide a handy wrap-up for your baby. Or wear a waterproof apron.

- Use a hooded baby towel to keep your baby warm and cozy after a bath. Warm your baby's towel near a radiator or heat vent.

- Drape a large, dry towel over your baby's infant seat. Place your baby in the seat and wrap the towel around him immediately.

- Keep bath items handy by storing them in a plastic, handled toolbox near the tub.

- Remove potentially dangerous items from the tub or sink area. By four months, your baby will have the interest and ability to grab everything within reach.

Bathing Routines

- Keep the time babies are undressed to a minimum. When they're older, they can better regulate their body temperature.

- Turn down the thermostat on your hot water heater to 120°F, to prevent your baby from being accidentally scalded. Run the cold water last so the faucet won't be hot if your baby touches it.

- Use even mild baby soap sparingly on your baby's skin. (Ivory is a strong soap; Dove and Neutrogena are better choices.)

- Bathe your baby by holding her facedown (face out of the water) in a frog-like position with your hand supporting her chest and tummy.

- Use only warm water to wash your baby's face. Be careful to keep soapy water away from eyes.

- Set the plastic bottle of baby soap in the tub water so it will be warm when you're ready for it.

- Remove cradle cap by gently scrubbing your baby's scalp with a soft toothbrush or very soft hairbrush and a little baby oil or vegetable oil. Or soften the scales by applying baby oil or petroleum jelly at night and washing them off in the morning with a soapy washcloth. Make sure to check behind the ears for "crusties."

- Put any powder you use into your hand first, away from your baby's face, so the powder particles aren't inhaled by your baby. For the same reason, don't let an older baby play with an open powder container. Many doctors discourage the use of baby powder because the inhaled particles may irritate a baby's lungs.

Diapering

Don't worry if you missed the parenting class on diapering. Parents quickly become experts who not only can—but do—change diapers in their sleep.

Cleaning Baby's Bottom

Some parents like the convenience of premoistened wipes, but there are lots of options.

- Make your own inexpensive wipes by soaking small paper napkins or sections of double-ply toilet tissues in a shallow bowl of baby oil. After the oil is absorbed, store the wipes in a plastic bag or covered container. If the wipes are drying out near the top of the container, store them upside down.

- Dampen cotton cosmetic pads with water, and store them in a zip-lock bag.

- Keep a roll of toilet paper, soft paper towels, or a box of tissues near the changing area

- Use Handi Wipes. They rinse out easily and can be reused.

- Recycle old cloth diapers by ripping them into smaller pieces and using them as wipes. Toss them in the laundry with the other cloth diapers.

- Wipe a soiled bottom with a cotton ball dipped in baby oil.

- Keep a small spray bottle filled with water near the diaper area to make a messy diaper area easier to clean.

- Change your baby's diaper on the bathroom vanity. Lay your baby on a towel, hold his legs up, and scoot his bottom to the edge of the sink for easy cleaning. Never take your hands off your baby in such a place.

- Color-code washcloths if you use them as wipes. Use one color for bathing, another for diapering.

Diapering Tricks of the Trade

- Keep a roll of masking tape handy to mend diaper covers and torn tabs on disposables.

- Cover a baby boy's penis with your hand or a diaper to avoid being sprayed. Point the penis down before securing the diaper, to direct the stream where you want it to go.

- Keep a radio or CD player near the changing table, to soothe a fussy baby.

- Hang a mobile near the changing table, preferably one that plays a song while rotating.

Using Cloth Diapers

Diaper covers, which make cloth diapers easier to use, are available with Velcro closures or snaps, eliminating the need for pins. Several styles are available, including waterproof covers that go over cloth diapers and one-piece wraps that have the diaper already attached.

Velcro closures tend to collect lint, however. Periodically remove the lint with a stiff toothbrush or lint brush, or brush the rough tabs against each other. For diapers without built-in closures, diaper clips are available. If you choose to use diaper pins, keep the following in mind.

- Only use diaper pins with plastic-covered ends. Never use ordinary safety pins.

- Place your fingers between your baby's skin and the diaper to avoid poking your baby with a pin.

- Wrap a wrist pincushion around the top bar of the crib or changing table. (Move it to a safer place when your baby is old enough to reach for it.)

- Stick pins into a thick potholder or decorative candle for storage, or hang closed pins on a cup hook screwed into the wall.

- Run pins along a bar of soap to help them slide through diapers more easily, or run them over a strand of your hair or across the top of your head.

- Attach a few pins to your key chain so you'll always have ones handy.

- Don't hold pins in your mouth. Babies are great imitators!

Preventing Diaper Rash

Experienced parents may smile at the thought of "preventing" diaper rash. It seems almost every baby gets it at some time or another.

- Change your baby's diaper often.

- Avoid wipes that contain alcohol; they can dry out your baby's skin.

- Avoid rubbing your baby's bottom too hard or too much. Always pat dry or air-dry.

- Gently air-dry your baby's bottom using a hair dryer set at "warm." Make sure to hold it at least ten inches from your baby's skin.

- Let your baby's bottom air out for a minute or two at each changing.

- Bathe bottoms even when not giving a full bath.

- Avoid fabric softeners and other laundry products that may irritate your baby's skin. Babies are often sensitive to softener buildup, and overuse makes cloth diapers less absorbent.

- Don't use diaper covers that don't "breathe." They prevent evaporation and increase the risk of diaper rash.

- Smooth on a light coating of zinc-oxide cream after every diaper change. Petroleum jelly is also effective, as is vegetable shortening. (A rubber spatula is good for applying these moisture barriers.)

- Store petroleum jelly or diaper cream in a plastic squeeze bottle to make it easier to handle.

- Use wedge-shaped makeup sponges to apply diaper cream or petroleum jelly, to keep your hands clean and to prevent diaper tabs from getting greasy.

Treating Diaper Rash

Once your baby has diaper rash, you try one thing...and then another. Many doctors oppose "greasing" a baby with oils and lotions, and experienced parents don't apply creams or ointments too thickly. "More is better" doesn't always apply here.

- Consider disposables if you've been using cloth diapers—and vice versa. The change often helps. Or switch to a new brand of disposables.

- Use unscented, hypoallergenic wipes if your baby seems to be having a problem with regular wipes.

- Exposure to air can also help treat diaper rash. Allowing your baby to nap bare-bottomed and facedown (when old enough) on a folded diaper might do the trick.

- Use half a capful of Mylanta on the rash area every other time you change your baby's diaper. It's great for babies with sensitive skin.

- Crush an antacid tablet (like Tums) and mix it with petroleum jelly to make your own worth-a-try diaper rash cream.

- Fill a spray bottle with sixteen ounces of water and half a tablespoon of baking soda. Shake the bottle to dissolve the baking soda. Spray your baby's bottom and gently wipe clean. Blot the skin dry and apply ointment or powder before applying a new diaper.

- Soak your baby's bottom in an Aveeno Oatmeal Bath.

- If serious diaper rash persists, talk to your baby's doctor about a stronger topical remedy.

Setting Up the Changing Area

You may find it practical to set up "satellite" changing areas around your home. Keep them stocked with diapers, wipes, clothing, and other essentials. Or store changing supplies in a container that can be carried from room to room.

- Use decorative kitchen canisters to hold baby items near the changing table.

- Use the top of a dresser for a changing table. Cut an old belt in half and staple the ends to the top of the dresser to make a safety belt for your baby. Line the drawers with wrapping paper from your baby shower gifts.

- Make cleanup easier by keeping a waterproof pad on your changing table. If the pad gets wet or soiled, toss it in the laundry. Or cover your changing pad with a pillowcase that can be easily removed and laundered.

- Sew two bath towels together to cover your changing pad. Make several covers so one will always be ready.

- Hang a shelf or two near the changing area to keep diaper supplies handy and out of children's reach.

- Use a three-tiered, hanging mesh basket for storing necessities, or use a wall hanging with pockets for small articles. A shoe bag works well, too.

- Hang a mesh laundry bag near the changing table for baby socks, breast pads, and other small items. Run the whole bag through the wash to keep small items from getting lost.

- Keep a Thermos of warm water near the changing table to avoid stumbling around in the dark at night and to avoid running water for what seems like hours to get the right temperature.

- Save time by folding cloth diapers only as you need them. Keep a laundry basket of clean, unfolded diapers near the changing area.

- Keep two diaper pails near the changing area: one for soiled diapers and the other for soiled clothing that will be transferred to the laundry. If you use cloth diapers, keep the container half-filled with water, and add some borax so it doesn't get smelly.

- Cut down on cleaning chores by using plastic liners inside the diaper pail.

- Use a Diaper Genie or similar device to store soiled disposable diapers without any smell.

Other Uses for Baby Wipes

- Cleaning tender episiotomy sutures
- Wiping down bathroom surfaces
- Cleaning scrapes and bruises
- Soothing mild sunburn
- Blotting spills and removing certain stains, especially in cars
- Wiping a toilet-training toddler (only the flushable wipes)
- Removing eye makeup
- Cleaning hands after pumping gas
- Keeping babies and toddlers clean in the car or at a restaurant

Baby Laundry

Parents are often surprised by the amount of laundry a tiny person can generate. If you're using cloth diapers, make sure they're not only clean but germ-free, to help prevent diaper rash. Many parents opt for a diaper service, especially in the first few weeks or months with a new baby.

Cloth Diapers

- Empty stools in the toilet and rinse out the diapers (even those that are only wet) before putting them in the laundry.

- Sprinkle a little baking soda or borax in the diaper pail to keep soiled diapers from souring.

- Soak soiled diapers overnight in the washing machine with soap and a commercial soaking solution. Run them through the regular cycle the next day. Add a second rinse cycle or run them through again without soap for a good rinse.

- Keep cloth diapers soft and fresh-smelling by adding a handful of baking soda to the first rinse cycle. Fabric softener is expensive and may irritate your baby's skin.

- Try an old-fashioned diaper softener and whitener: vinegar. A cupful in the second rinse gets rid of soap and helps prevent diaper rash.

- Instead of bleach, use a quarter cup of ammonia in the diaper pail or laundry. It works great and doesn't eat up diapers like bleach does.

- Use an inch or so of kitty litter or baking soda at the bottom of the diaper pail to absorb odors. Change the litter once a week to keep it fresh.

- Rub a little baby oil on plastic diaper covers that are becoming dry and brittle, or add a little baby oil to the rinse water.

Stained Clothes

- Soak stained clothes or mildewed hand-me-downs in hot water with a half cup each of vinegar and laundry soap.

- Soak stained clothes overnight in hot water with a cup each of laundry detergent, bleach, and dishwasher detergent. Finish the wash cycle in the morning, run a second warm cycle, and give them an extra rinse to make sure all the bleach and detergent are removed.

- Use a moistened cloth dipped in baking soda to dab soured dribbles on your baby's clothes.

- Carry a stain remover stick in your diaper bag, or keep one near your changing area to apply to stains before they set.

- Remove formula stains from color-fast clothes by dipping a toothbrush in Murphy's Oil Soap and scrubbing the stain out.

- Remove formula stains from white clothes by wetting the stain and sprinkling it with scouring powder containing bleach or baking soda. Brush it out with a toothbrush.

Ready-to-Go Baby Bag

Keep your baby bag stocked so it's always ready. Fill it with diapers, wipes, a changing pad (or a two-foot square of washable vinyl wallpaper), an extra set of clothes, a few small toys, a snack or two, a beverage for your baby, and zip-lock bags (or a roll of plastic bags and twist ties) for soiled diapers. Pack a clean bottle set and some dry formula. (Fill the bottle with water if you're breastfeeding.) In winter you may want to add a baby blanket and a pillowcase for keeping blanket lint off your clothes. In summer you may want to add sunscreen, sunglasses, and baby bug spray. Consider saving the free samples of baby products you received in the hospital. (The containers are usually refillable.) Leave room for your wallet and keys so you don't need to carry a purse, or carry your personal items in a fanny pack.

Creating a Stimulating Environment

Gradually, your entire home will become child-oriented, but your baby's room will probably be the most entertaining play area. Babies learn through play, so provide an environment that's both safe and stimulating. A newborn is only able to focus on objects eight to twelve inches away, but by three months a baby is able to focus on objects a few feet away.

Stimulating Your Baby

Use as much color in your baby's room as you like (wall paint, curtains, wall hangings, patchwork quilts, printed crib sheets, and so on). Infants see red, yellow, and black-and-white images best, and they love faces, especially ones with prominent eyes. Dress your baby in bright, patterned outfits, and put them on yourself occasionally for fun and to stimulate your baby.

- Decorate a wall with a montage of baby congratulation cards, or frame some cards to hang separately.

- Fasten bright decals on the insides of the bassinet, crib, and stroller. Make sure you remove them before your baby is old enough to pull them off and put them in his mouth.

- Hang pictures of smiling babies. Babies seem to recognize and love these faces.

- Hang some cute plastic place mats or other decorative items on the wall.

- Put a colorful poster, kite, or piece of wallpaper on the ceiling above the changing table. Or hang an inflated punch ball balloon.

- Place a small corkboard near the changing table so your baby can enjoy your older child's artwork.

- Hang your baby's development calendar near the changing table to record major milestones and other significant moments.

- Keep a music box in your baby's room, or hang wind chimes outside your baby's window.

- Put your baby's infant seat in locations that allow him to see as much of the household activity as possible without being in danger.

- Put a mirror tile at floor level on the wall in your baby's room— fun for your infant now and for your crawling child later!

- Hang some toys and rattles on your baby's crib using snap-on shower curtain rings. Or attach the rings to an infant seat or car seat in place of more expensive plastic play links. The rings can be also used to lock cupboard doors when your baby gets mobile.

- Cut off sections of old socks or tights that have multicolored bands, and use them as baby wristbands. As your baby moves his hands, the colorful wristbands will capture his attention.

- Use Velcro strips to attach small stuffed animals to the changing table or horizontal crib bar.

- Decorate your baby's room with brightly colored potholders. They're safe and can eventually be used in the kitchen.

- Decorate your baby's highchair with colorful pictures and decals. Cover them with a clear, protective material (such as Contact paper) to help them last longer.

- Baby mobiles are terrific, but they can be a danger once a child can stand and grab them. After six months or so, move them to ceiling hooks to keep them out of reach.

- Entertain your baby with a wadded ball of transparent tape. Make sure the ball is larger than a toilet-paper tube so your baby can't swallow it or chew pieces off.

Saving Money on Equipment

It's not necessary to buy every piece of equipment for your baby. There are many workable substitutes, especially in the first few months when your baby is changing so quickly.

- Use a travel crib for a comfortable, portable bed. The travel crib can also function as a playpen. If you can't bring the portable crib when traveling, have your baby sleep in a laundry basket, baby bathtub, or dresser drawer lined with a firm pad.

- Let a carriage serve as an infant bed. It can be gently rocked, unlike a crib.

- Use a small, inflatable plastic wading pool as a playpen for a child who's not yet crawling. Make sure the sides can't be collapsed from within.

- Make an outdoor toy storage container out of a large plastic plant pot.

- Place a carpet remnant inside your baby's playpen for warmth and cushioning. The remnant will be durable and fairly easy to clean.

Siblings

Older children will no doubt be excited at the prospect of a new baby. If you're still pregnant, you'll want to explain where the baby is (in Mommy's uterus—where the older child once was). Talk about how the baby will cry, nurse, sleep, and take a lot of your time. Make sure your older child doesn't expect an instant playmate!

Preparing the Older Sibling

- Move your older child up a step or two before the baby arrives (to a big bed from a crib, to another bedroom, to preschool for a day or two a week), so these changes won't be misconstrued as rejections after the baby arrives.

- Babysit a friend's or relative's baby at home to let your older child see what things will be like. You can refresh your baby skills, and the baby's parents will owe you.

- Take your child to the hospital and explain what will happen while you're there. Visit the nursery and have lunch in the coffee shop. It will be good for your child to know where you are when you leave to have your baby.

- Take your older child to a prenatal checkup to hear the baby's heartbeat. Have your doctor or midwife answer any questions your child may have.

- Let your older child help pick out a present for the baby (and one for himself or herself).

- Shop together for new outfits for the baby (and ones for the older child).

- Have older children draw pictures for the baby's room using bright markers on white poster board. Frame the drawings or hang them with pushpins. Make sure the children sign their names, with help if necessary.

- Have your child talk to the baby using your navel as a microphone.

- Make sure Dad or your partner is actively involved with your older child, or whoever will frequently be in charge of your older child after the baby comes home.

- Don't start any of this too early! Nine months is an eternity to a child. Consider waiting until the second trimester or later, if possible.

While You're Gone

- Tape-record some stories for your child to listen to while you're in the hospital.

- Leave a photo of yourself in your child's room.

- Prepare some gifts to be given to your child while you're gone.

- Ask your older child to take care of something special for you while you're at the hospital (perhaps a scarf or piece of jewelry).

- Call your child frequently from the hospital or birth center, especially if children are not allowed to visit.

- Let your older child bring small treats to school, such as granola bars or suckers wrapped in pink or blue ribbon, to pass out to classmates to announce the birth.

- Avoid carrying your new baby when you first arrive home or when greeting your older child at the hospital. Let someone else hold the baby so you can devote some reunion time to your older child.

Helping Siblings Deal with Jealousy

It's important to understand that the trauma of a rival is very real for a child. Jealousy may not appear until your child is older or the baby becomes mobile, but you should be prepared for it.

Don't expect your older child to love the baby instantly. Make it clear that hurting the baby is not allowed—but that adoration is not required. Have your baby "bring" your older child a gift from the hospital (perhaps a shirt that says "Big Sister" or "Big Brother"). Keep a few gifts on hand for your older child when visitors bring gifts only for the baby, or when your child has helped with the baby.

- Schedule one-on-one time with your older child each day.

- Express your occasional annoyance with your baby's demands, but not so often that your child gets the idea that the baby is a permanent nuisance. Express your joy, too.

- Put a stool next to the changing table so your older child can watch you change diapers and dress the baby.

- Put a photo of the big brother or sister near your baby's crib, so your older child can see how important he or she is to your baby.

- Create a special basket of toys that comes out only when you're feeding your baby. Or watch a videotape with your child while feeding your baby.

- Let your older child help as much as possible with "our" baby by getting things for you and by singing, talking, and otherwise entertaining the baby.

- Set the crib mattress at the lowest point so your older child won't be tempted to try to pick the baby up.

- Stall visitors who come to see the baby, so your older child can be the center of attention for a while. Show photos of your child as well as the baby. Let your older child help you show off the baby.

- Expect some regression from your older child; try not to pay much attention to it. Your older child may suddenly want foods served in a baby food jar, for example.

- Praise your child for any positive behavior such as waiting patiently, sharing toys, or helping with the baby. Or give the child new privileges such as a later bedtime, increased allowance, special things to do with a parent, and so on.

- Teach your older child that smiling often at the baby will "teach" the baby to smile.

The Other Kind of Sibling

To help your family pet adjust to your new baby, bring home one of your baby's undershirts or receiving blankets before you bring your baby home. Give it to the pet to play with and sniff, so your baby's odor will become familiar. Consider "pet-proofing" your baby's room by installing a gate across the door. You'll be able to look in and out, but pets will be kept out. Never leave your pet alone with a new baby.

Doctor Visits

- Keep a notepad handy to write down any questions you want to ask your baby's doctor at checkup time. Jot down observations regarding your baby's sleeping, crying, eating, and elimination patterns.

- Don't be afraid to ask your doctor anything. There's no such thing as a foolish question.

- It's a good idea to write down any verbal instructions you receive from your doctor. What seems perfectly clear in the office may be less clear when you get home.

- If you normally use cloth diapers, consider using a disposable for a doctor visit. That way you won't have to take a soiled diaper home.

- Bring washable markers for your older child to play with while waiting for the doctor. Have your child draw on the disposable paper that covers the examination table.

When Your Child Is Afraid of the Doctor

- Bring a favorite doll or toy animal for the doctor to examine first.

- Buy or borrow a toy doctor kit for your child to play with at home. You can be the patient, or have your child "examine" a favorite doll or stuffed animal. If you're receiving a shot, make sure to cringe—but remind your child that this will help you become healthy and strong.

- Be honest. Let your child know that it (whatever procedure) will sting for a minute but will be over quickly.

- Perhaps a different doctor, even within the same group practice, would be a better choice.

Reasons to Call the Doctor or Nurse Hotline

- The first occurrence of any illness new to your baby, even a cold

- Diarrhea (bowel movements more frequent and watery than usual)

- Constipation that lasts for several days

- Blood-tinged urine or bowel movements

- Poor feeding (baby stops the usual vigorous sucking during feedings)

- Relentless or unusual crying, including a hoarse, husky cry

- Significant changes in skin color, breathing, behavior, or activity

- A rectal temperature of 101°F or higher

- Listless behavior, especially if your baby is usually active and alert; unusual drowsiness that lasts a long time

- Convulsions, "fits," or spells involving stiffening or uncontrollable twitching

- Fluid draining from your baby's ears; ear pulling or constant turning of the head; crying when coughing

- Projectile (forceful) vomiting; green vomit

- An unfamiliar, serious-looking rash

- Redness or discharge from the eyes

- Any injury in which the pain or disability doesn't disappear after fifteen minutes

- Symptoms that may indicate an adverse reaction to an immunization, such as fever, swelling at the injection site, rash, and relentless crying.

Returning to Work

Parents who are planning to return to jobs outside the home after paternal leave should start thinking about childcare and postpartum help while they're still pregnant. It's important to have backup plans if your original plan doesn't work out. Be flexible and keep your sense of humor; no one balances work and family without hitches. Remember, returning to work involves two separate but equally important tasks: 1) leaving your child, and 2) reentering the workplace as a productive employee.

Prior to Your Return

- Call your boss and coworkers to get caught up with what's going on. Have important memos and e-mails sent home.

- Try to stop by your workplace for a few short visits before your leave ends. Bring your baby along to introduce to your coworkers. Also consider inviting your nanny, if you have one, so she can see what your work environment is like.

- Set up a meeting with your boss to talk about what you'll be doing when you get back and to help you organize your schedule. Maybe there's a project you can do by e-mail to make reentry easier.

- Journal your feelings for a week and note any changes in yourself.

- Cook and freeze several meals so dinner will be easier to handle.

- Talk to your partner about chores and the division of labor, including dropping off and picking up your child if you're using daycare. Remember, this is a team effort.

- Select a pediatrician or family doctor convenient to either your daycare facility or home. Let your travel time and work hours determine the location, if possible.

- Start bringing your child to daycare part-time for a week or two before going back to work. This will help your child adjust to the new environment and will give you time to run errands and get other things done.

- Plan to introduce a bottle when your baby is three or four weeks old, if you're breastfeeding and want to continue providing breastmilk when you're not available. Have someone else give the bottle, since your baby will probably refuse it from you. Make arrangements to buy or rent a breast pump, and think about when and where you'll use it.

First Days Back at Work

- Plan a light schedule for your first week back, if possible, or consider a part-time reentry schedule. It will give you and your child time to adjust.

- Parents sometimes experience grief when faced with the reality of leaving their baby at daycare. These emotions will soon pass once you realize your child is being well cared for and is happy to see you at the end of the day.

- Start back midweek. Some people find it hard to jump back on Monday and work a full week right away. Or phase back gradually by working shorter weeks the first month or so, if possible.

- Join a support group of parents in your workplace, if one's available. Or think about starting your own. Check with your employer. All you need is an available room once a week (or month) over lunch hour and an invitation to others with infants or young children.

- Show your coworkers that you can still do the job. People will be watching to see if you're really committed.

- Call your daycare provider or sitter as often as you need to in the early weeks.

- Don't worry if you feel slightly jealous of or competitive with your child's caretaker. It's normal. Remember that babies always know who Mommy and Daddy are.

- Keep your office clothes clean in the morning by wearing an oversized shirt while feeding and changing your baby.

- Bring home extra work each day. If you have to stay home with your child unexpectedly, you can work while your baby's napping.

- You're still entitled to private time even when you go back to work. You may have to find it by rising before your children or by having your partner or sitter take over for a while. Use your private time to refresh your inner self, and resist the temptation to get chores done. Everyone in your family will benefit.

Chapter 2

Child Care: The Basics

The routines of feeding, clothing, and getting your child to sleep move slowly from things you do for them to things you help them do for themselves. While it often seems easier to do it all yourself, you'll want to encourage as much self-help as possible.

Feeding

If you worry about getting your baby to eat, don't. It's not really possible. You can control the quality and variety that you offer, but your baby should control the quantity eaten. Be aware that children's appetites usually decrease dramatically at about one year of age because their growth slows. As for your child's attitudes, respect strong food dislikes. Your job is to provide preferred, nutritious foods. Your child should determine how much is eaten.

Feeding Your Baby

- Warm baby food in an egg poacher using the compartments for different foods.

- Use paper muffin cups or coffee filters for appropriate baby foods, to save on dish washing.

- Purée foods in a blender, food mill, or food processor, and freeze them in ice cube trays or in "plops" on cookie sheets;

then transfer them to plastic bags. Cubes thaw quickly and are easy to take along for meals away from home.

- Use a spoon to feed a young child a banana right out of the peel, one bite at a time. The rest of the banana will stay fresh.

- Make your own baby oatmeal by placing rolled oats in your blender or food processor. Cook the fine, flour-like cereal with water or milk until it's the right consistency.

- Serve sugared cereals as an after-dinner treat.

- Add a little liquid to soft-cooked meats to make them easier to grind in a baby food grinder. In the same grinder, you can purée most of your table foods (unseasoned) for your baby.

- Use a long-handled spoon that fits your baby's mouth. Plastic-coated spoons feel good on tender gums.

- Keep your baby from sliding down in a highchair by putting a small rubber sink mat (or nonslip bathtub daisies or strips) on the seat. Even a square of non-adhesive foam or rubber shelf lining works.

- Use a fabric highchair insert that attaches to the back of the chair and ties around your child. It helps a very young child sit up while holding the child securely in place. It's good for travel, too, as it can turn a standard high-back chair into a highchair.

- Use a plastic booster seat as a highchair when you're planning to be away from home during mealtime. Strap the booster seat to a regular seat and buckle your baby in safely.

When There's No Highchair or Booster Seat

To "trap" a small child for feeding, cross your left leg over your right knee at the ankle, forming a triangle. (Reverse the position if you're left-handed). Set your child in the triangle. A child can't get out and can't squirm. You can even take a few bites of your own meal while feeding your child. Or use the stroller, infant seat, or car seat for feeding.

Bibs

- Use a molded plastic bib with a bottom "lip" that provides a good catchall and becomes its own feeding tray. They're the best! Or try to find a bib with cap sleeves to keep your baby's clothes clean. If the bib isn't waterproof on at least one side, save it for drool and dribble.

- For an inexpensive, durable, easy-to-clean bib, use a kitchen towel with crocheted, snap handles that hang from the refrigerator or stove (and fit nicely around your baby's neck).

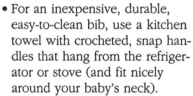

- Make an instant disposable bib from a plastic handled grocery bag. Cut an inch or two off the bottom, cut up one side between the handles, and have your child slip her arms through the handles.

- Use an apron or an old T-shirt. (You can always find cheap ones at garage sales.)

- Sew old or inexpensive vinyl bibs to the backs of terry cloth bibs to make them waterproof. Your baby's chin will be protected by the soft terry cloth.

- Pin a fabric bib to your baby's clothes for better coverage.

- Tuck a double thickness of facial or toilet tissue under the neckline of the bib to keep drools from running down your baby's neck.

- Try a colorful bandanna on a child who's a "bib resister." It's also a cute option for a heavy drooler.

- Use clip clothespins to attach a dishtowel or napkin to clothes, especially for an older child. It will keep clothes clean but won't make the child feel like she's wearing a bib.

41

Gnaw-Ons for Teethers

Most children are bothered to some extent by teething, although discomfort levels vary. Most babies begin drooling around three months. This is not necessarily a sign of teething, nor is fever a normal part of this process. Pressure seems to soothe sore gums and help teeth erupt more efficiently. Consider the following teethers:

• A cold or frozen bagel (Beware of chunks a baby might gum or bite off and choke on.)

• A chilled navel orange cut into sections, or unpeeled chunks of apple or other fruits (Caution, as above.)

• A cold or frozen carrot or stringless cold celery (Caution, as above.)

• A frozen banana, or a piece of banana cut lengthwise (Caution, as above.)

• The core of a fresh pineapple, cut into quarters (The core is not as strong-tasting as the rest of the fruit, but it still may be a bit too acidic for some babies.)

• Frozen teething rings or chilled pacifiers

• A dampened washcloth or soft potholder, frozen and stored in a plastic bag

• A toothbrush

• A clean rubber canning ring

• A gum-numbing product (like Orajel) lightly applied to any of the previous four items

• An ice cube tied in a washcloth with a short, secured string

• A bottle nipple filled with frozen water (To achieve this, freeze a small bottle with a small amount of water upside down. Keep the bottle attached to the nipple so the ice will melt into the bottle and not on your baby.)

• A new, clean rubber ring from the puppy department of your supermarket or pet store

• A dog biscuit (Really! They're not harmful in any way! Caution, as above.)

Do-It-Yourself Eaters

Self-feeding is messy, and it often takes a child a long time to eat even a small meal, but you should encourage it anyway. Don't panic if your child prefers fingers to spoons; they're faster, and the feeling of food is as important to a child as its color and flavor. The finer points of etiquette can be picked up later. Just make things as easy as possible for your child (and yourself).

• Put a rubber-suction soap holder on the highchair tray to keep the plate or bowl from slipping and to free your baby's hands for eating. Or use a plate that comes with suction holders on the bottom. Or use a weighted plastic pet bowl. It's heavy (hard to toss or turn over) and unbreakable!

• Pile your baby's food directly on the highchair tray to avoid the thrown plate.

• Give your baby a spoon in each hand, and use one yourself. Your baby will imitate you. Demitasse or small sugar spoons and hors d'oeuvre forks (not sharp ones!) are easier for babies to handle. For a real beginner, consider a wooden tongue depressor as a food scoop.

• Give a child who insists on eating from a big plate a plastic one with a raised rim. Many have divided sections.

• Give a butter spreader or plastic picnic knife to a child who wants all the tools grownups have.

• Mashed potatoes are a good first food for self-servers, since they adhere to utensils.

• Rinse large-curd cottage cheese in a colander with running water. The remaining large pieces make a perfect finger food.

• Roll banana slices in graham cracker crumbs or toasted wheat germ to make them less slippery to pick up.

• Give a child an empty flat-bottom ice-cream cone to eat. It dissolves slowly and doesn't produce a lot of crumbs.

- Mix dry cereal with yogurt, cottage cheese, or applesauce (instead of milk) for a child who hasn't mastered a spoon yet. Or make hot cereal very pasty so it stays on the spoon.

- Spread puréed meats on whole wheat bread, and cut into finger food servings.

- Minimize spills by giving your child a straw for sipping cooled soup, and save the spoon and fork for fruits and veggies.

- Allow extra time for a self-feeder.

- Feed a self-feeder right before bath time.

Entertaining with Other New Parents

Serve your adult guests finger foods that can be eaten with one hand. Many of them will have a baby on one arm!

Do-It-Yourself Drinkers

If you're bottle-feeding, slip a brightly colored sock or wristband over the bottle to make it easier for your baby to hold. Wrapping a few rubber bands or a bathtub appliqué around the bottle will serve the same purpose. When weaning a child to a cup (sippy or otherwise), begin by reducing bottle feedings and by asking your child to help you deliver bottles to another baby who needs them. Or take the nipple off the bottle and let your baby drink from the lip of the bottle. You may also want to cut the nipple off the bottle and tell your baby the bottle is "broken." Your baby will soon be convinced. Or offer water in a bottle and juice in a cup. Juice usually wins out.

- Let your toddler learn to use a regular cup by practicing in the bathtub. (Don't let your child drink the bath water though!)

- Use the tips mentioned in the paragraph above to make a regular drinking cup easier for little hands to hold.

- When young children no longer want to drink from a baby cup or sippy cup, give them commuter cups to use. They hold more and spill less, and they make a child feel grown-up.

- Fill cups only about a third full to prevent waste from tipping or dropping, until your child is more skilled.

- Let your child drink from a plastic medicine cup or eyewash cup. They're easier to hold and won't soak your child if spilled. Or try three-ounce paper cups.

- Let your child use one or more bright-colored straws for drinking from a glass, cup, or can. Cut the straws off two inches above the top of the container to help prevent tipping.

- Turn around the tab on a canned drink so it's over the opening, to help hold a straw in place.

- Use any of the ubiquitous bottles with pop-up tops. (They're also refillable.)

- Turn the little plastic bear in which honey is packaged into a fun drinking container. Rinse it thoroughly, and cut the upper end to the diameter of a drinking straw. (Tie a bow around its neck for a great party favor!)

- Use a clean, empty, cap-topped yogurt cup for an almost spill-proof container for kids. Put a hole in the center of the lid for a straw.

- Assign each of your children a specific cup or mug to avoid washing excess dishes or wasting paper cups. Have children rinse their cup in hot water and place it upside down on the drying area for next time.

Easy Eating

- Quickly cool many foods that are too hot for a toddler by dropping an ice cube into them or by placing them in the freezer for a minute or two.

- Serve bran muffins slightly frozen. They're nutritious and produce fewer crumbs.

- Mash leftovers, mix them with an egg, and cook like them like pancakes or bake them in muffin tins.

- Thicken watery soups by adding instant potatoes a little at a time while cooking.

- Substitute vanilla ice cream when you're out of milk. It works well with waffles and hot cereal.

- Give your little one grated cheese. It's the perfect size for little fingers, and it's ready to serve when your child can't wait.

- Make a sandwich easier for a toddler to handle by using Pepperidge Farms Very Thin Bread slices.

For Older Tots

- Let your child choose breakfast by dividing favorite dry cereals into individual servings and placing them somewhere that's easily accessible. Alternate with individual packets of instant oatmeal and Cream of Wheat. (Convenient and nutritious.)

- Help your children get their own breakfast by putting out a lidded bowl of cereal and placing glasses of milk and juice in the refrigerator. All they do is pour the milk over the cereal.

- Help your child learn to use chopsticks by making them easier to hold. Fold up a small piece of paper and place it between the chopsticks at one end. Then wind a rubber band around the paper and chopsticks to secure the end.

- Require your child to eat the same number of bites of vegetables as her age. (A younger child can feel special for having to eat less, and an older child can feel important for eating more.)

- Make a list of "yes" foods your children can munch on without asking you (bananas, apples, carrots, water chestnuts, raisins, rice cakes, and so on).

- Provide fussy eaters with a small mirror to watch themselves eat. A little entertainment may help get the food down.

- Prevent foods from touching each other (if your child gets upset about this) by using separate bowls or plates with dividers. Kids eventually outgrow this phase.

- When you need to serve several pointed-bottom cones at once, stand them in a block of Styrofoam in your freezer.

Creative Containers

- Let your hungry child have a paper bag of small goodies he can pull out and eat while you prepare a meal.

- Give your child cereal or soup in a plastic cup or mug with a handle. The remaining milk or broth can be drunk instead of spooned out.

- Use a molded ice cube tray to chill Jell-O Jigglers (a.k.a. "Knox Blox") for ready-to-eat snacks.

- Fill the compartments of a muffin tin with different finger foods such as cheese cubes, strips of cold meat, crackers, raw vegetables, or fruit. Call it a "potpourri lunch."

- Serve an occasional meal on a doll plate, an aluminum pie plate, or a new Frisbee, just for fun.

- Fill an ice-cream cone (flat-bottom works best) with tuna salad, egg salad, cottage cheese, yogurt, or fruit. It makes a good on-the-run lunch or fruit snack for an older child.

- Put your child's favorite lunch foods in the refrigerator crisper bins. Save yourself time by having your child pack his own lunch with the foods found there.

- Make children's sandwiches using hot-dog buns, which are easier for kids to hold.

- Serve Sloppy Joes in unsliced burger buns. Slice off the "caps," dig out the excess bread, fill, and recap.

- Use wooden Popsicle sticks to serve anything from a hot dog to an apple section.

- Use refrigerator biscuits to make peanut butter and jelly sandwiches for little hands.

- Wrap a flour tortilla around a hot dog for a change of pace. Add grated cheese and microwave for 30 seconds. Add guacamole, sour cream, or salsa for a Mexican flavor.

- Fill flat-bottom ice-cream cones half full with your favorite cake mix. Bake on a cookie sheet at 350°F for 20 minutes. Cool, frost, and top with a maraschino cherry. For a birthday, add a scoop of ice cream on top. (You can cook two cones at a time by microwaving for 45 seconds.)

Creative Design

- Let a preschooler construct a "dangerous dinner" by using toothpicks to hold together pieces of meat, chunks of cheese, vegetables, dried fruits, or anything good. When it's "built," it's ready to eat.

- Slit hot dogs lengthwise one to three times into narrow strips before serving. If you slice a raw hot dog only two inches from one end and cook it in boiling water, the strips curl up and it looks like an octopus! Avoid cutting hot dogs into small circular pieces that can block a child's windpipe if not well chewed.

- When apple pieces are too slippery for your child to hold, peel and core a whole apple and have your child hold it by slipping a thumb or finger through the center.

- Arrange pieces of fruit in a fun design on top of your child's cereal.

- Create designs on dinner foods using broccoli for tree tops, shredded carrots for hair, half a cherry tomato for a nose, peas for eyes, and so on.

- Cut up certain foods with cookie cutters, and decorate with faces.

- Use a pizza cutter or canapé cutter to cut spaghetti or pancakes into bite-size pieces. Cut Popsicles in half and trim bread crusts for those who won't eat them.

- Enhance your preschooler's sense of independence by letting him cut his own food.

- Use a ready-made refrigerated pie crust that can be unfolded when your kids want to make cookies and you don't have time. Pull out the cookie cutters, sprinkle the dough with sugar sprinkles or cinnamon-sugar, and bake.

- Hide treats in the cabinet in an empty oatmeal container. Kids never think to look there.

Strategies for Food Jags and Picky Eaters

Don't panic. The calories and servings that authorities recommend for children's health and growth are averages. Some kids burn more calories; others less. Learn substitutions. Serve smaller portions. Offer healthy snacks. Don't keep sweets around. Find "good" fast foods. (While most are high in salt, fat, and calories, some, such as pizza, have a higher nutritional value.) Avoid fighting about food. Make up the difference with vitamins. Substitute vegetables with fruits. Give up what you can't control.

- Let your child choose one cereal (usually sugared), and you choose another (unsweetened). Mix the two and serve for breakfast as a compromise.

- Serve inexpensive, low-sugar cereals topped with a tiny bit of any of the following: coconut, candy sprinkles, one or two gummy bears, chocolate drink mix, a few chocolate chips, or a little premixed sugar and cinnamon.

- Add a few drops of vanilla extract and food coloring to milk, for a child who won't drink the regular stuff. Serve it as a milk shake with a bright colored straw.

- Have your child help prepare a meal by dropping food in the food processor and pressing the button. Finicky children are more inclined to eat food they've helped prepare.

- Sprinkle shredded cheese over veggies to make them more appealing.

- Add a bit of blue food coloring to applesauce to make your own "Blues Clues" food.

- Add some green (or blue) food coloring to scrambled eggs to make your own "Green Eggs and Ham!"

- Don't assume food rejected three weeks ago will be rejected now.

- Put sugar in an aluminum flour shaker for a child to use when adding sugar to cereals. It eliminates spills, avoids the problem of too much sugar in one spot, and makes it easier to cut back on sugar use.

- Use condiments to make nutritious foods more appealing. Put ketchup on peas, add ranch dressing to veggies, use dips for green beans, and so on.

- Disguise important nutrients in meatloaf, hamburgers, or spaghetti sauce by adding pureed vegetables or baby food to them. Pureed cauliflower can be added to mashed potatoes.

- For additional ways to cope with finicky eaters, read my *Taming of the C.A.N.D.Y. Monster* (Book Peddlers, 800–255–3379).

Treat Tricks

- Avoid messes by putting a Popsicle in a disposable cup trimmed to half its original size. Make a slit in the bottom of the cup, insert the stick, and have the cup catch the drips. Coffee filters work well, too.

- Fill a balloon with your child's favorite juice. Put a Popsicle stick in the hole and tie. When frozen, cut away the balloon for a giant Popsicle!

- Use transparent tape across the cup top to hold Popsicle sticks upright when making flavored ice in paper cups.

- Make "cookie pops" birthday treats by inserting Popsicle sticks into cookies before baking. Frosting is optional.

- Have your child frost cupcakes with a wooden Popsicle stick. It's safe to lick when the job is done.

- Minimize leaks by putting a marshmallow, malted milk ball, or banana slice in the bottom of a cone before adding ice cream.

- Pour flat soda into an ice cube tray to make "tasty pops."

• Freeze leftover candy from Halloween and winter holidays. When summer rolls around, have your kids set up a leftover-penny-candy stand.

Cleanups: Your Child

• Carry your baby to the sink using the football hold (tucked under your arm), and make a game of washing hands and face after meals.

• Put baby oil or petroleum jelly on your baby's face before feeding, to facilitate cleanup.

• Use only your hand dipped in water to wash the face of a reluctant child. Most children won't fight a hand as much as a washcloth, and you'll do just as good a job.

• Gently spray your child's hands and face with water from a spray bottle, and wipe clean. Kids love it.

• Warm a soft, wet cloth or baby washcloth in the microwave for a few seconds before cleanup. Check before using to make sure you haven't made it too hot.

• Let your child dip messy hands in a plastic bowl of water while still in the highchair. Then wipe dry. Hold onto the bowl so it doesn't get tossed.

• Squirt a little shaving cream on your child's cheeks, and then "shave" it off with a washcloth.

• Remove a drink mustache by dabbing toothpaste on it and rinsing it off. Kids usually like the pleasant taste and smell.

• Keep a step stool handy for a child old enough for washing hands and face at the sink.

• Use baby wipes for after-meal cleanups. Not only do they remove normal food stains (think grape juice), but wipes containing alcohol are good for ink and magic-marker stains.

Cleanups: Equipment

• Put a plastic tablecloth or an old plastic shower curtain under the highchair for easy cleanup. Or spread out a section of newspaper and pull off one page after each meal (wrapping the crumbs inside). Or get a nonfinicky dog!

• Mount a plastic paper towel holder on the back of the high-chair for quick cleanups.

• Rub waxed paper over the runners of a clean highchair to make the tray slide on and off more easily. Or apply some petroleum jelly, vegetable oil, or WD-40.

• Cut a plastic place mat to fit the shape of your highchair tray to make it easier to clean.

• Clean a highchair tray by adding a few drops of shampoo your toddler can play with after eating. When your child tires of finger painting, simply clean the tray and the child with a wipe of a sponge.

• Place a plastic or metal highchair in the shower, and let hot water spray all over it for a few minutes. Caked-on food wipes off easily.

• Clean a highchair outdoors with a garden hose. Let the high-chair sit in the sun for a time to help disinfect it.

• Give your child an ice-cream pail and sponge, and enlist "help" in the cleanup.

• Use a paper towel as a place mat to make table cleanup easy.

• Get rid of stains on dishes, cups, and countertops by using a spray bottle filled with a mild bleach solution (make sure to label it) or baking soda.

Clothing

Begin to give your child choices about clothing as soon as possible. Having a few options can make all the difference with a finicky youngster. For one who doesn't care, it provides practice in making decisions. Choosing an outfit will also enhance your child's self-image. Necklines in slip-over clothing must be large enough to slip over your child's head without a struggle. Preschoolers need plenty of pockets for collecting things. And remember, front fasteners will be easier for your child (and for you when you're the dresser).

When You're the Dresser

- Buy overalls with snaps in the crotch for easy diaper changing.

- Name clothes as you put them on and take them off.

- Play games such as "Peek a Boo" and "Where Has Your Arm Gone?"

- Use a barrette to clip straps from jumpers or overalls closer together at the back (to prevent them from sliding off your child's shoulders). Or fasten them with mitten clasps. Or criss-cross and pin them where they overlap.

- Run a bar of soap (the little ones from hotels are ideal) or a lead pencil over a sticking zipper.

When Your Child Is the Undresser

Don't be surprised if the toddler you just dressed removes all clothes within minutes. That's a skill to be mastered, too. (One-piece garments, often called onesies, will help discourage undressing.)

- For babies who like to take their diapers off, use elastic waist pants to cover the diapers. Or put diapers on backward so the tabs are on the back side, making them harder to undo.

- Consider switching to cloth or pull-up diapers. They can be harder for a child to remove.

- Prevent your child from unzipping clothes by securing the zipper lead to the garment with a diaper pin.

- Put a child's one-piece sleeper on backward at night. You'll probably have to cut off feet coverings, however.

Featuring Footed Items

- Apply T-shaped pieces of adhesive tape or nonslip bathtub appliqués to the bottoms of footed sleepers, socks, or slippers to give more traction and help a young walker gain confidence.

- If footed sleepers are too warm for your child's feet, use a hole puncher to provide ventilation in the soles.

- Make sock or sleeper bottoms skid-proof by painting them with a pen or tube of paint that dries in a raised design.

- Slip sport wristbands or hair bands around the ankles of too-long pajamas. Make sure they're not too binding.

Nighttime Diapering

- Use overnight diapers if you're using disposables, or double diaper your baby or toddler if you're using cloth diapers.

- Put a sanitary pad (or part of one) inside a diaper.

- For a female toddler who sleeps on her stomach and leaks through disposables, use "boy" diapers that are extra absorbent in the front.

- Pull-up disposables are available for older children who still wet at night.

- Roll up a disposable diaper long ways (with the absorbent side facing out), and place it inside a cloth diaper like you would a sanitary pad.

- Put a Velcro-closing cloth diaper over a disposable if the disposable leaks at night.

Changing an Active Child

- Reserve a special toy that comes out only at changing time. Give it to your baby the moment he lies down.

- Cover a baby wipe container with pictures of baby faces cut from magazines. Babies love to look at faces of other babies.

- Change your baby in front of a children's video or television show like *Sesame Street*.

- Install an inexpensive, shatterproof mirror near the changing table at your baby's eye level. Your baby will watch the mirror while you enjoy a hassle-free diaper change. Or put up mirror tiles.

- Talk to your child dramatically. This brings attention to your face, not your hands.

- Let your child play with a toothbrush or a wadded ball of masking tape. These keep fingers and interest occupied. Make sure the ball of tape is larger than the inside of a toilet paper tube.

- Let your child play with a small flashlight during a diaper change.

- Dress a squirmy toddler facedown, if you can, for better control.

- Try dressing your child on your lap instead of a changing area.

- Learn to change diapers on a pad on the floor or while your child is standing.

- Let your little one diaper a favorite doll or stuffed animal first. Then it's your child's turn.

- Entertain your child by singing a favorite song or reciting a nursery rhyme.

- Use a hand puppet to do the work and amuse your child during changing or dressing. Use it to tell a story and get the job done simultaneously.

- Have your child hug you while you change the diaper.

- Let your child pick the location for a diaper change. Having some control over the situation may be all your child needs to cooperate.

- Bring the clothes to your child when the opposite isn't working.

- For a toddler who frequently refuses to lie still for a change, consider switching to pull-up diapers that can be changed standing up.

- Give an older child advance warning about the need for a diaper change. It will help prepare him for a disruption in play.

- When all else fails, tickle, tackle, and move very quickly!

For a Tot on the Crawl

- Put socks or booties on your crawling baby's hands, if you're at a beach or someplace similar, to allow mobility while making it impossible to pick up and eat forbidden things.

- Use sport wristbands to protect a crawling baby's knees.

- Overalls and stretch suits stay in place better than separates that might get left behind as crawlers begin moving about.

Save Time...Save Pajamas

If you can bring yourself to break old habits at bedtime, dress your toddler in tomorrow's loose-fitting clean clothes instead of pajamas. Today's fabrics don't wrinkle, and your child is ready to go in the morning.

Dressing Themselves: Zippers and Fasteners

You'll want to encourage your child's every effort at self-dressing, even though it takes much more time and often causes frustration for both of you. Keep yourself busy nearby, and be ready to help out if needed.

- Make button handling easier by sewing large buttons on your child's clothes wherever possible. Make it easier yet by sewing them on with elastic thread.

- Teach your child to button from the bottom up, to improve the chances of coming out even.

- Tie large buttons or small toys securely to hood strings, to keep them from being pulled out.

- Attach notebook rings or key rings to zipper leads on boots and jackets, to make them more manageable. On boots, the rings can be hooked together for storage.

- Teach your child to pull a zipper *away from* clothes and skin, to keep it from catching or pinching.

- Help sticky snaps work easier by spraying each side with non-stick vegetable spray.

Dressing Themselves: Other Helps

- Buy pants and skirts with elastic waistbands that are easy to pull on and off. Make sure the elastic isn't so tight that it makes an imprint on your child's skin.

- Use a piece of masking tape or adhesive tape (or an indelible marker) to mark the belt hole a child should use.

- Try to find clothing with monograms, appliqués, or special designs on the front to help your child tell the front from the back. On homemade items, mark an X on the back with colored thread, or add an appliqué.

- Teach your child to look for the label on the back of underpants. If there's no label, indicate the front by sewing on a "belly button" or drawing one with an indelible marker.

XYZ!

Is your boy often caught with his zipper down? Say, "XYZ!" ("Examine your zipper!"), and, "PDQ!" ("Pretty darn quick!").

Outerwear

- Put a small treat (Raisin, Cheerio) into your children's hands so they'll make a fist to push through a sleeve (and be rewarded once the sleeve is on).

- Sew loops of elastic thread inside the cuffs of sweaters, and have your child hook them over thumbs to hold sleeves down while putting on a coat or jacket.

- Attach mittens to a long string that goes through both coat sleeves, if your toddler can undo mitten clips.

- Use knee-high socks as mittens to make them harder to pull off.

- Clip mittens together with clip clothespins to keep track of them when not in use.

- Attach wet mittens to a hanger with clothespins; hang to dry.

- Put a pair of surgical gloves or dishwashing gloves over regular gloves to keep them dry and warm for an older child.

- Encourage your child to slip one mitten or glove inside the other after taking them off. When you find one, you find the other.

- Hang a snowsuit to dry, or toss it in the dryer. To prevent "fill" from clumping, throw a tennis ball or a sneaker into the dryer with it.

- Insulate boots, or make them fit better, by cutting a piece of carpet or Styrofoam (from a food tray) to fit the inside sole.

- Use a portable hair dryer to dry winter boots quickly.

- Help your toddler put on a jacket or coat independently. Spread the garment on the floor front side up. Have your child stand at the neck end, bend over, slip arms into the sleeves, and flip the coat over her head. Or have your child lie down on the garment face-up, put arms into the sleeves, and then stand up.

Putting Shoes On

- Put shoes on a squirmy toddler while your child is in the high-chair. Or lightly tickle the bottom of your child's foot; toes will uncurl and shoes will go on smoothly.

- Use mitten clips to attach your baby's shoes to the pants hem. If shoes are kicked off, they aren't lost.

- Wet your child's shoelaces before tying them. As they dry, they'll tighten up and stay tied. Better yet, look for shoes with Velcro fasteners.

- Prevent the tongues of shoes from sliding out of place by cutting two small parallel slits in each tongue, a half-inch from the outside edges. Insert the laces through the slits and tie as usual. Many are made that way today.

- Put plastic bags over shoes or socks before putting boots on, for ease of entry. The bags will also help keep shoes and socks dry.

- Cover shoes with large woolen socks to keep your child's feet extra warm and dry inside boots. Buy boots large enough to accommodate the extra layer.

Helping with Shoes

Shoes aren't necessary for new walkers. Going barefoot gives little feet good exercise. For a child a little older, new shoes are often a source of great pleasure. They can also be a source of frustration.

- Place nonslip bathtub appliqués or pieces of masking tape on the soles of slippery shoes. Or apply a small amount of glue in a zigzag pattern using a glue gun. Some shoe bottoms can be given extra traction by rubbing them with sandpaper or scoring them with the tip of a scissors.

- Periodically trace your child's footprint on a piece of sturdy cardboard. Carry it as a guide when you're shopping without your child and find a great shoe bargain. You should be able to slip the footprint into the shoe.

- Write your children's names on the bottom soles with a permanent marker. If their shoes are ever in a pile with others, it'll be easy to find them.

Left from Right

- Help your child distinguish between the right and left shoes by marking the inside edges of both shoes with tape or a colored marker. When the marks face each other, the shoes are on the right feet.

- Explain to your child that if the toes point in, shoes "like each other" and are happy; if they point out, they're sad.

- Mark the inside heel soles with an L and R or a design to match up shoes in their proper position. Or draw a design on the front of sneakers (one-half on each shoe) so the puzzle matches up.

Lacing Tips

- Coat the ends of shoelaces with clear nail polish, or wrap them with masking tape when the plastic tips wear off.

- Tie knots in shoestrings after the first two holes are laced, or tie knots near the ends of the laces so your child can remove the shoes but won't be able to pull the laces out.

- Avoid lacing and tying problems by substituting quarter-inch elastic for laces. Sew ends together at the top. The elastic stretches so the shoe can be slipped on and off without untying.

- Keep shoelaces even at the ends by tying knots at their centers.

When Teaching a Toddler to Tie Shoes

- Tie a black lace and a white lace on sturdy cardboard.
- Practice on a large shoe with laces.

Keeping Clothes Organized

- Hang coordinated sets of clothes in the closet, or put complete outfits together in bureau drawers so your child can select matching items.

- Pin together outfits that have more than one piece, so you'll never have to worry about which item goes with which outfit.

- Organize socks for more than one child by assigning a special pattern or color to each child, or by buying a different brand for each.

- Buy all socks in the same brand and color for an only child, to save the trouble of matching them.

- Use large pins to keep pairs of tiny socks together for laundry and storage, and for pinning to the clothesline.

- Identify children's clothes with an indelible pen, a liquid embroidery pen, an inexpensive rubber stamp, or a fabric paint pen.

- Write names on dark-colored boots and rubbers with red nail polish or a cotton swab dipped in bleach. If you prefer to mark inside the boots, use a marking pen.

- Use small, hanging pocket bags, shelves, or drawers for storing shoes.

- Sort clean laundry into colored baskets. Assign each family member a color, so each person knows which pile of laundry to fold and put away.

Hand-Me-Downs

- Mark borrowed clothes that need to be returned, and label things you lend and want returned, by writing the owner's initials on the clothing tag with an indelible pen.

- Sort hand-me-downs according to season and size, and label the containers in which they're stored. Use disposable diaper boxes, plastic containers, or bags that designate weight or size. Preserve precious baby things (ones you want to save forever) in self-closing plastic bags or plastic containers with sealing lids.

- Make boys' hand-me-downs feminine by embroidering initials on pockets and designs around collars or cuffs. Or sew on appliqués or lace trim.

- Change hand-me-downs so they're special for your child.

- Mark your oldest child's clothes with a single X or dot, mark your second child's clothes with two Xs or dots, and so on. When clothes are handed down, it's easy to add another mark.

- Mark sizes on the inside waistbands of pants, if labels have come off or are unreadable.

- Use a last name only for marking outer clothes you're sure will be handed down from one child to another.

- Avoid resentment over hand-me-downs by calling them "hand-me-overs," "kindergarten dresses," "first-grade pants," and so on (instead of "Susie's dresses" or "Jimmy's pants"). Encourage your younger child to think of hand-me-downs positively.

Shopping Wisely

Some of the best-dressed children have the least amount of money spent on their clothes. Garage sales, thrift shops, discount stores, and manufacturers' outlet stores account for considerable savings. Many thrift shops will take your children's used clothing for sale on consignment. Hand-me-downs from relatives and friends also help. Clever shoppers try to keep a little cash on hand for an unexpected opportunity. Carrying a small notebook with measurements and sizes of all family members helps, too. For small children, height and weight measurements are often more important than sizes. Remember to update your notebook often.

- Don't buy plastic pants with snaps; they rip off too easily.

- Buy "neutral" jeans, shirts, and outer clothing so they can be passed on to children of different sexes.

- Get unisex clothing in boys' departments; it's usually more rugged and often costs less than items in girls' departments.

- Buy best quality on everyday wear, such as underwear, and in items that will be passed on to several children.

- Check for fit in socks (if you aren't sure of the size) by having your child make a fist and wrap the sock around the fist over the knuckles. If the heel and toe meet, the sock will fit.

- Buy tube socks. They wear evenly, are easy to put on, and "grow" with kids.

- Buy shoes with laces or Velcro closings for small children. Slip-on shoes are cute and easy to put on, but they often don't stay on.

- Try two-piece grow-a-size pajamas. If you always stick with the same color and brand, you can use good parts of worn-out ones for patches.

- Consider using bright T-shirts with iron-on transfers or embroidery for nightshirts.

- Buy smock-type dresses for girls; when they get too short, they can be worn as tops over pants.

- Buy two-piece snowsuits for better value; one-piece suits may be easier to put on, but two-piece suits can be worn longer.

Home-Sewn

"Get a good sewing machine and learn to use it, and learn to knit and crochet," is the advice of many parents who want their kids to be dressed well and economically. Work ahead of the seasons: Think about hats, mittens, and jackets in the summer, shorts and sundresses in the winter. Don't put hems in until it's time for kids to wear the garments.

Allow for growth by choosing styles with undefined waistlines (in one-piece garments) and raglan or dolman sleeves. If you make double-breasted coats and jackets, you can realign buttons as your child grows.

- Accurately measure children for clothing by laying them on their backs on the material; measure or pin the length of arms and legs.

- Always wash fabric before cutting, to allow for shrinkage and bleeding of colors. Use the water temperature and drying method you'll use for the finished garment.

- Sew on shank buttons and metal overall buttons with dental floss to keep them from being torn off.

• Use snaps wherever possible; they're often easier to manage than buttons.

• Apply clear nail polish over the tops of small buttons to help keep them from coming off and perhaps finding their way into a small child's mouth.

• Avoid sewing on buttons when you know you'll be moving them as your child grows. Instead, sew thread through button eyes as if you're sewing the button onto cloth. Attach the buttons to the garment with safety pins run through the thread on the back, and repin as needed.

• Sew an extra button under the hem of a front-buttoning garment, so you'll have a matching one when the garment is lengthened.

• Sew an extra button or two to a piece of fabric from a garment, and store it in your button box for easy replacement.

• Use cellophane tape or masking tape when you're measuring and marking hems; it won't pinch or stab your child as pins will.

• Save handwork by using iron-on bonding materials for hems in lightweight fabrics.

• Put a long zipper from top to crotch in overalls for a boy who's toilet trained. A standard fly is usually hard to manipulate.

• Use empty vitamin bottles or other small containers with child-proof caps to store pins and other little sewing notions. Contents are easily visible, yet safe from children.

Other Uses for Velcro

• In small circles down the fronts of shirts and blouses (instead of buttons)

• For waistband closures

• To attach overall straps to overall bibs (instead of buttons)

• To keep mittens together for storage

• To keep belt ends in place

• To keep overall straps from slipping down a child's arms

- To keep a dress shirt "tucked in" by using button tabs at the pants waistline

- On washcloths or pieces of fabric, to make easy-to-change diapers for your child's doll

- To make a "custom" T-shirt that your child can attach tiny stuffed animals or toys to

- To attach small toys to the walls as decorations

Making Clothes Last Longer

- Buy two-piece sleepers for longer wear; when they're too short, extend their lives by cutting the feet off.

- Open the bottom seam of an outgrown one-piece blanket sleeper, and use it for a beach coverup.

- Try tie-dying T-shirts that are badly stained.

- Put extra buttons on overall straps at longer lengths than your child needs. As your child grows, the old ones can be snipped off. Sew double rows of snaps or buttons on two-piece sleepwear for the same reason.

- Lengthen girls' slacks by sewing on strips of grosgrain ribbon or decorative braid. Add similar trim or ruffles to the bottoms of pajama pants, or cut off sleeves and legs to make summer pajamas.

- Lengthen suspender straps by sewing on extra fabric.

- Add another tier to tiered skirts or jumpers, using matching or contrasting fabric.

- Cut the too-short sleeves off of an expensive quilted or padded jacket, and let your child wear it as a vest over a heavy sweater.

- Extend the wear of jackets and snowsuits by sewing knitted cuffs (from the notions departments in fabric stores) to the ends of the sleeves.

Patching and Covering Up

- Patch the knees and feet of blanket sleepers with pieces of an old, flannel-backed tablecloth.

- Cover old hemline marks on skirts or pants with zigzag stitching or sewn-on rickrack or ribbon bands.

- Run a dark blue crayon or indelible pencil over the white line on let-down jeans.

- Slip a rolled-up magazine into pant legs to avoid running through both thicknesses of material when pinning on patches. Or hold patches in place for stitching by gluing them on first. After sewing, wash the glue out.

- Sew on an appliqué to cover a hole, mend, or stain that shows.

Knit Knacks

- Crochet mittens onto the sleeves of a sweater so they'll never get lost or separated.

- Choose a pattern one size larger than your child needs when you're preparing to knit or crochet a garment. If it takes a long time to finish, there's a better chance it will still fit.

Preventive Maintenance

- Spray fabric protector on the knees, cuffs, and collars of your child's garments (and the fronts of "best" clothes for a drooler or messy eater). Spills will bead up, and dirt can be wiped off with a damp cloth.

- Sew squares of quilted material on the knees of pants for crawling babies, to protect both pants and knees. Use iron-on patches *inside* knees—even on tough pants.

- Put iron-on patches on the cotton soles of sleepers to keep them from wearing out.

- Reinforce the knees of new jeans (on the inside) with iron-on patches or the extra fabric you trim from pant legs.

Getting Clothes Clean

Today almost everything but the child goes into the washing machine. Bleach of one kind or another does wonders with really dirty clothes. Some parents change brands of laundry detergent occasionally, feeling that the new brand washes out the residue of the old, and clothes get cleaner. If you take your laundry to a laundromat, carry your detergent in old baby food jars or self-closing plastic bags to lighten the load. And remember, there's no law that says kids' play clothes must be spotless!

- Get grimy socks white by soaking them in a solution of washing soda and water before laundering. Yes, bleach works, too. Or boil them in water with a sliced lemon.

- Soak egg-stained clothing in cold water for an hour before laundering. Hot water will set the stain.

- Soak vomit-stained clothes in cold water, and sponge stains with a solution of a quart of ammonia and a half teaspoon of liquid detergent.

- Use bottled rug shampoo with a brush (and lots of suds) for winter coats that need dry cleaning. It works on both wool and corduroy.

- Pour boiling water through grape-juice-stained areas of clothing over a sink or bowl.

- Place a piece of waxed paper over gum on clothing or fabric. Run a warm iron over the area to "melt" the gum onto the waxed paper. Or use masking tape to lift it off.

Kid-Created Stains

Something our parents failed to mention (or we chose to ignore) is the joy and frustration of continual laundry. Parents need to become experts in stain removal and in keeping mounds of clothing in motion.

Over the years, various people have recommended the following items for stain removal. I won't vouch for each of them. Often their effectiveness depends on the nature of the stain, how old it is, and the nature of the fabric. The following list includes options you may want to try. One or more may work for you.

Ballpoint pen/ink:
Hair spray
Toothpaste and toothbrush
Vinegar on painted surfaces

Crayon:
Goo Gone
WD-40

Blood:
Hydrogen peroxide
A paste of meat tenderizer
Shampoo rubbed in, then cold water wash
Whink Wash Away
Goo Gone

Grass:
Alcohol
Shampoo
Simple Green
Tilex Soap Scum Remover
Soak overnight, then wash with bleach
Toothpaste and toothbrush
Whitewall tire cleaner
Whink Wash Away

Grease:
Baby/talcum powder, then brush off
Baking soda
Club soda
Crisco
Go Jo
Oven cleaner
Goo Gone

Spills/stains:
Baby wipes
Baking soda
Bleach on a cotton swab
Club soda
Liquid dishwasher detergent
Murphy's Oil Soap

Oven cleaner
Rubbing alcohol
Shaving cream
Toilet bowl cleaner
Toothpaste and toothbrush
Upholstery cleaner
Window spray

You can find a lot of information on stain removal on the Internet. Use your favorite search engine and type the words *stain removal*. One site worth checking out is www.crayola.com/canwehelp/staintips/stain.cfm. Many of the websites run by commercial companies claim their product alone is good in every situation. My preference is to try baking soda first, as a paste or sprinkled on. It can't do any harm, and you can always try something else if it doesn't work. Many products like Oxiclean and other "orange" based cleaners are excellent stain removers.

Caring for Shoes

- Clean white baby shoes by rubbing them with a raw potato, liquid nonabrasive cleaner, or alcohol before polishing. Or apply toothpaste with an old toothbrush, scrub gently, and wipe off. Let shoes dry before polishing.

- Spray newly polished white baby shoes with hair spray to prevent polish from coming off.

- Use baby wipes to remove black marks from white shoes.

- Remove gum from the bottom of shoes by putting them in the freezer. Scrape the gum off when it's frozen.

- Make white canvas shoes white again by washing them and polishing them with white shoe polish. Let them air-dry.

- To keep the soles of shoes from being stained with polish, paint the edges with clear nail polish.

- Use hair spray on stains on tennis shoes. Spray, leave for a few seconds, and wipe with a soft cloth. Or try toothpaste and a toothbrush or a soapy scouring pad. Use bleach or lemon juice in the rinse water if the shoes are white. Even foam bathroom cleaner can be effective on leather sneakers.

* Spray new sneakers with Scotchgard fabric protector to keep dirt from becoming embedded. Grass stains and mud will come out easier. Spray after every wash.

* Clean the bottoms of children's tennis shoes by using an old toothbrush or potato scrubber. Rinse under warm water.

* Dry out wet tennis shoes overnight by placing them on their sides in front of the refrigerator. The fan should produce constant warm air to dry them.

Sleeping

Getting children to sleep comfortably and fearlessly through the night is a challenge most parents face at one time or another. Just wait though—teenagers usually sleep very well, and often late into the morning when you'd like them to be up and about.

Determining Bedtime

* Try to keep the *same* bedtime every night to help establish regular sleep habits.

* Avoid bedtime confrontations by letting the hands of the clock do the job, or use a timer to enforce bedtime. Give your child time to prepare by issuing advance warning. Leftover time can be added to the bedtime ritual as a reward for cooperation.

* Have a "Goodnight Parade" for two or more children. The family marches through the house stopping in the kitchen for water, the bathroom for toothbrushing and toileting, the living room for locking the front door, and so on. The "caboose" (youngest) gets dropped off first.

* Have your child put all toys and stuffed animals to bed, saying, "Good night" to them one by one; when they're all down, your child can be the *last* one to go to bed.

Helping Children Get to Sleep

- Continue the sleep routine you started when your child was an infant. Or create a new routine. But do have a routine.

- Use the five- or ten-minute check for the child afraid to be left alone at night. After putting your child to bed, agree to come back every five or ten minutes until he's asleep. Knowing a parent will be back helps a child relax. Or work or clean up in the next room so your child can hear you nearby.

- Feed your older child a protein snack before bedtime, if you offer a snack at all. (Milk is protein.)

- Have quiet time before bedtime. Rough-and-tumble play excites a child, making it hard to settle down to sleep.

- Put a few favorite dolls or stuffed animals in your child's bed, and tell him the toys are ready to go to sleep.

- Let even a young child "read" himself to sleep with a pleasant book and maybe an accompanying audiotape.

- Don't use a crib or bed as a place for punishment.

- Put soft stereo headphones on an older child, and let restful music induce sleep. Make sure the headphone wires are on top of your child's head, not around his neck. Or set a clock radio that will turn off on its own.

- Give your child a relaxing massage.

- "Plant a garden" when giving your child a back rub. Use different strokes for spading, raking, preparing the rows, and planting the seeds your child selects.

- Encourage your child to relax every muscle, starting with his toes and moving toward his head. Eyes should be kept closed.

- Put a dab of cologne on the back of your child's hand. Sniff the scent until it's gone. Or put a few drops of a relaxing essential oil (like lavender or chamomile) in a bowl of warm water in your child's bedroom. Deep breathing and concentration usually bring sleep quickly.

- Write an idea for a pleasant dream on a slip of paper, and place it in a Dream Jar (an empty can or bottle you've decorated). Have your child reach into the Dream Jar to find the paper. Read the dream idea together, and have your child go to sleep with the paper beneath his pillow.

- Help your child decide what to dream about (a favorite game, an upcoming event, a relative, and so on) as part of your bedtime routine.

- Take a long walk with your child in the evening, followed by a nice warm bath and some soothing music.

Bedtime Storytelling

- Relate a true event about your child or your family (the day you were born, what you did as a child, the day your child was born, and so on).

- Tell a story using one of your child's favorite dolls as a hero.

- Tell a story in which your child fills in important details. For example, "You and I were ready to cross the street, and (your child fills in the blank)." Remember to keep stories short and the central character familiar, since children's attention spans are limited.

- Tell a story in which your child is the hero (such as "Lady Dana and Sir Douglas"). Adapt common childhood stories, create new ones using your imagination, or replace names in picture books with your child's name.

- Check out specially printed, personalized books that incorporate important names from your child's life (siblings, friends, pets, and so on).

- Use liquid paper to erase characters' names in storybooks, and fill in your children's names.

When Going to Sleep Is Problematic

Some parents let a wakeful child cry after checking to make sure there's nothing wrong. They say the crying becomes progressively shorter over a few nights, and eventually stops altogether. Check your clock rather than your gut feeling. It always feels as if children are crying longer than they actually are. If you can't bear to do that, keep in mind that rubbing a child's back or giving reassurance from the door every five minutes will often do the trick. Avoid picking up or rocking your child after three to six months of age, or giving an unnecessary bottle. Children have to learn to calm themselves for sleep. If you choose to do it for them, they'll continue to let you.

- Give your child a bottle, if you wish. If your child has teeth, prevent tooth decay by giving water only or by brushing after milk or juice.

- Keep several pacifiers in the crib, but never tie one to a string around your baby's neck or crib bar. The string may get tangled around your baby's neck and cause strangulation. You can tie one to a short (four-inch) ribbon securely sewn to a stuffed animal, making it easier to find during the night.

- Keep your child near you at night. One "family bed" option is a king-size bed with a one-side-removed crib pushed up against it. Another is a guardrail on one side of the bed; the parents needn't be separated with a child between them, yet there's no worry about the child falling out of bed. For some, family sleeping equals comfort. Those who like the idea (not everyone does!) say it fulfills a basic human need for warmth, closeness, and security.

- Use an incentive chart to encourage an older child to stay in bed. Draw stars on a calendar for each night your child doesn't come to your bed. (Let your child choose the color.) Ten stars might earn a small present.

- Put a crib mattress, futon, or a big pillow on the floor near your bed for the nighttime waker who needs to fall back to sleep near you.

- Attach a car drink holder to the crib railing to hold a spill-proof cup of water. Your toddler won't have to wake you for a drink.

- Use a nightlight in your child's bedroom, or let your child have a flashlight. Or try a lighted fish tank, which offers not only light but movement and soft bubbling sounds. A bed light with a dimmer switch allows an older child to read a little and then go back to sleep without getting out of bed.

Delaying the Early Riser

- Put a few cloth books or soft toys in your toddler's crib for morning play. But do it after your child is asleep.

- Attach an unbreakable mirror to the inside of the crib so your baby or toddler can amuse himself for a few minutes in the morning.

- Leave a "surprise bag" (*never* a plastic one) by the bed of an older child, or fasten a bicycle basket or plastic pail to the side of the crib after your child is asleep. Fill the container with items for quiet play.

- Add a snack for a child who wakes up hungry and who can handle eating without supervision. One healthy, time-consuming snack is a Cheerios snake: Tear two to three inches of waxed paper from a roll; fold lengthwise; place a few Cheerios in the fold at one end, twist the paper to hold in the Cheerios; place a few more pieces in the next section of paper; twist the paper to hold in the Cheerios; continue until you have a "snake" or "necklace" full of Cheerios. Your child must untwist each section to get at the next batch of Cheerios. (Some parents won't put food out, feeling that it may attract undesirable animals or insects.)

- Set an alarm clock or clock radio for a child who *always* wakes early. When it goes off, the child may get up. Or set up two clocks for a preschooler (one running, the other not running and set at getting-up time). When the hands of the second match those of the first, the child may get up.

- Set up your TV/VCR/DVD with a favorite video your child can turn on in the morning. (Preset the volume down if you can.) Or set a small TV or radio to go on in your child's room when your child usually wakes up.

- Give up! Accept your child's body rhythms. Perhaps there's a twenty-four-hour grocery nearby, so you can do some shopping during those early hours.

Naps

- Try white noise in a little one's room, if older children's playing keeps your younger child from sleeping. Set up a small fan on a high dresser, direct the airflow away from your child, and let it hum away.

- Make a naptime nook for a toddler by decorating a large cardboard box with bright drawings or decals. Pad it comfortably.

- Help slow your child down for a nap by placing a bird feeder near the bedroom window for your child to watch.

- Let an older child nap in a sleeping bag on your bed, the family room couch, or the floor of your child's room, just for variety.

- Call naptime something else, such as "rest time" or "quiet time," for a child who resists sleeping. Sometimes the child will actually fall asleep; but if not, the time will still be relaxing.

- Set a clock radio to play quiet music for a resting child, or put on a soft audiotape or CD. The end of the music marks the end of rest time. Children usually drop off long before the music does.

- Read a book or two to your child as part of a naptime routine.

- Have a toy that can be played with only at naptime.

- Wake a too-long napping child to the sound of favorite music.

Going Visiting?

If the friend you're visiting doesn't have a crib, and your *nonmobile* infant needs a nap, there are several options. In addition to the infant seat, stroller, or car seat, a bed can often be found in the bathtub! Lay your baby face-up on a pad/baby blanket with a bath rug or a few soft towels underneath. Make sure to remove soap and other bathing equipment, just in case!

Chapter 3

Hygiene and Health

Parents of young children usually spend a good deal of time in the bathroom...but not by themselves! Trying to keep active kids clean, introducing them to the art of cleaning themselves, and getting them to use the toilet are time-consuming operations. Here are some ideas to make that time pay off.

Soap and Water

When there are two or more little bodies to be bathed (or even just one), many parents find the assembly line method fast and easy. One parent washes and shampoos; the other dries and assists with pajamas.

Bathing and Shampooing

- Use a clean plastic syrup bottle or dishwashing detergent bottle as a baby shampoo dispenser. The pull-up top lets you squirt just the right amount and close it with one hand. Or keep baby shampoo in a hand-pump soap container labeled with a permanent marker. It allows you to keep one hand on a slippery baby at all times.

- Take your child into the shower to get him used to water on his head and face.

- Strap your baby into an infant seat with a towel over the pad, if you use a big tub for your baby who can't sit alone.

- Place your baby bathtub in the regular tub when your baby is not big enough to sit up in a bathtub. It helps keep an active infant in place and your floor dry.

- Let a child who can sit upright do so in a bathtub ring seat or a small, mesh plastic laundry basket in the big tub. The water flows into the basket while your child remains contained. The empty basket can also serve as a place to store bath toys when the bath is finished.

- Try using a plastic inflatable pool in the shower stall, also as a transition.

Removing Grass Stains

To get rid of summer grass stains on little feet, rub each foot with half a lemon for about a minute or so.

Making It Fun

- Wear a puppet washcloth on your hand to make face cleaning less traumatic.

- Give your child a "smelly" bath using kitchen flavor extracts. Peppermint extract is fun. A little food coloring adds interest to the water experience.

- Help teach a little girl to get herself clean in the tub by pretending she's a big girl getting ready for a party. Soap on the face is cream, powder, blush, and eye makeup; soap on a leg is a silk stocking; soap on an arm is a white satin glove; shampoo is hair spray; and so on.

- Create a fun, washable bath mitt out of an unmatched sock. Draw a face with a permanent marker to make it a puppet.

- Buy bath towels that depict your child's favorite book or television characters.

- Use colored sidewalk chalk or bathtub crayons for drawing and coloring in the tub. They wash off easily.

Play in the Bath

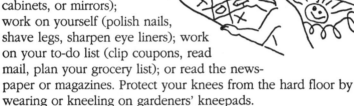

There are many bathroom activities to keep you occupied while your child is happily at play in the tub. Clean the room (toilets, cabinets, or mirrors); work on yourself (polish nails, shave legs, sharpen eye liners); work on your to-do list (clip coupons, read mail, plan your grocery list); or read the newspaper or magazines. Protect your knees from the hard floor by wearing or kneeling on gardeners' kneepads.

- Store bath toys in a large plastic planter. They're sturdy, have drain holes, come in many colors, and are inexpensive.

- Keep bath toys in a nylon net bag, and hang it from a faucet, showerhead, or the wall (with suction holders) to drip dry.

- Turn other toys into bathtub toys occasionally, especially when they need a good cleaning.

- Toss small rubber bathtub toys in the washing machine whenever you launder your shower curtain. A little bleach will kill mildew and germs. Use the gentle cycle.

- Clean grungy bathtub toys by soaking them overnight in a bucket of water with a cup of bleach and a dash of detergent. Or periodically run them through the washer and dryer. (Avoid very hot water or high heat.)

- Make inexpensive bath toys by cutting colored sponges into interesting shapes.

- Let bath time be "science time." Provide a variety of things that sink and float, that are tall and thin—or short and fat (plastic glasses), that are large and small, that pour (measuring cups), and so on.

- Let bath time be snack time. A cookie can be a good distraction while you scrub your child clean.

- Save blowing bubbles for the bath. There's no mess or residue left on floors or furniture.

- If your toddler hates to leave the tub, pull the plug. When there's no more water for play, the bathtub will lose its interest. Or set a timer to let your child know when bath time is over.

- Make simple rules for bath time, such as, "You're through when you stand up," or, "You're through when your skin is wrinkled and you look like a raisin."

Bathtub Safety!

Never leave a small child unattended in a bathtub—even if an older sibling is present! A little one can drown in less than an inch of water.

Fear of the Tub

- Bathe with your small child to provide extra security. It's fun, too!

- Run the bath water before bringing a frightened child into the bathroom, if you don't have another child who might climb in while your back is turned.

- Ask questions to find out what's scaring your child. Is it the water? The drain? A slippery tub? Getting hair washed?

- Lure a child who's reluctant to get in the tub by putting creamy hand lotion in little cups and mixing a few drops of food coloring in each. Have your child use the concoction to "paint" his face and body, then have him hop into the tub.

- Create a diversion by having your child help you put the bath toys, bubble bath, or even a nonskid mat in the tub. Some parents prefer to use a little liquid dishwashing detergent for bubbles. (Commercial bubble bath has been known to contribute to vaginal infections in little girls if used too often.)

- Use only a few inches of water in the tub, increasing the amount as your child gets more comfortable with it.

- Swimming and swimming classes often help kids overcome bathtub fears.

- Let your child give a doll a bath in the tub. Exerting control over a fearful situation can help a child overcome the fear.

Making Shampooing Easier

Most first-time parents are surprised when a fear of shampooing develops, yet it's common. Shampoo as seldom as possible during this period. Once or twice a week is probably enough, unless your child has special problems. You can make a game out of hair washing by joining your child in the bathtub and pouring water over your head first. Or let your child wash a doll's hair while you wash hers. Don't force the issue or try to *prove* it doesn't hurt. Instead, brush your child's hair frequently (cover the brush with an old nylon stocking to help absorb oils), and occasionally wash hair with a damp washcloth. When you must shampoo, use a no-sting baby shampoo, and do the job quickly and matter-of-factly, praising your child for bravery. As difficult as this period is for both for you, remember that it too shall pass.

- Shampoo your child first, and then allow for playtime so the bath will end on a happy note.

- Try letting someone else be the shampooer (Dad, grandparent).

- Make shampoo sculptures in your child's hair. Keep a hand mirror nearby for your child to admire the new "do"!

- Try reintroducing a no-longer-used infant seat; the tilt allows the child's head to be tipped back comfortably for shampooing.

- Tell your child the story of a speck of dirt that gets tired, settles for a nap on your child's head, and is joined by lots more specks, only to get washed out by Mom or Dad. Telling the story should last as long as the shampooing.

- Sing loud songs together throughout the whole process.

- Wrap your child in a big beach towel, and have her lie face-up on the kitchen counter with head over the sink. Use a sprayer if one's available. The towel will hold your child steady, your closeness will provide security, and it will be easier for you to control the soap and water.

Keeping Shampoo Out of Eyes

- Put only a small amount of water in the tub so your child can lie down flat for shampooing.

- Fill a big plastic jug with water and let it sink to the bottom of the tub. Your child can use it for a headrest. Or use your arm to support your child's head.

- Have your child lean back under the faucet for a quick, easy rinse. Or make rinsing fun by using a watering can.

- Place colorful stickers on the ceiling over the tub to keep your child's attention during rinsing. Change stickers periodically if interest seems to wane.

- Use a sponge instead of a cup to control water when you rinse. (And try a sponge for applying shampoo. Soap won't be so likely to run into eyes.)

- Give your child a small folded towel or washcloth to hold over eyes and face. Or use a plastic visor. Create a disposable shampooing visor by cutting out the inside circle of a paper plate and placing it over your child's head.

- Use swim goggles to prevent soap and water from getting into your child's eyes. Make a game of it by telling your child she looks like a frog. Have your child repeat, "Ribbit!"

- Give your hands and sponge names, and have them argue over who's going to wash your child's hair.

- Let your child control the hand-held shower hose.

Removing Gum from Hair

Use peanut butter. Work it into your child's hair, comb out the gum and peanut butter, and shampoo. Cold cream works, too, as do olive oil and witch hazel. (Use baby oil to remove gum from skin, or press a second wad of gum over the first and lift both off together.)

For Girl's Hair Only

- Use transparent tape to attach a bow to a hairless baby girl's head. (This works on fine hair, too.)

- Iron hair ribbons by sweeping them through a hot curling iron.

- Decorate hair with yarn, long shoelaces, pipe cleaners, ribbon, and so on.

- Clip barrettes onto a long ribbon, and hang it in the bathroom or wherever you fix your child's hair.

- Slip hair ribbons through the coated rubber band before tying up your child's hair. The ribbons won't fall off and get lost.

- Wrap unused elastic bands around the handle of a hairbrush.

- Spray ribbons with hair spray to keep them stiff.

- Use spray-on conditioner after shampooing long, tangled hair. Or get in the habit of using regular conditioner after shampooing.

- Rub a sheet of fabric softener over static-ridden, flyaway hair.

- Distract your child while brushing her hair by counting the number of brush strokes.

- Braid long hair before bedtime to minimize tangles in the morning.

Clean and Neat

As children grow, they often begin to take pleasure in looking nice and smelling good. If they start out with serviceable habits, they're apt to stick with them. With babies and toddlers, the finer points of grooming are your responsibility, and you don't want to encourage self-help with such tools as scissors and cotton swabs.

Encouraging Good Habits

- Keep a sturdy step stool next to the sink to encourage self-help.

- Hang a small medicine cabinet on the bathroom wall at your child's eye level, to hold grooming necessities. If the cabinet has a mirror, so much the better.

- Buy mirror tiles to stick on the wall at your child's height. Position the tiles so you can add more as your child grows.

- Give your child an inexpensive plastic carrying case with his name on it. Equip it with personal hygiene items such as a travel-size tube of toothpaste, a toothbrush, a small bar of soap, and other necessities.

- Half fill your bathroom sink each morning with clean water. Let your child dip both hands in, soap up, and towel dry. Change the water as needed.

- Ask your child, "Are all those little germies gone?" This will help him conceptualize "stuff" that must be washed off.

- Give a bath mitt to a child who hates to wash up. Make one out of an old sock tied up with leftover pieces of soap inside, or sew two washcloths together after putting soap chips inside.

- Ask your child to wash a particular toy before a meal or after toileting. It's a good way to get hands washed without a battle.

- A liquid soap dispenser is probably *not* a good idea until children are about five and won't use it as a plaything.

Using Hand Towels

The best way to get really dirty hands clean is to have a child wash something in the sink: a toy, a doll, some plastic cups, and so on. Remember that a wet, dirty bathroom towel is better than a neatly hung, unused one.

- Assign each family member a color for towels and washcloths. Buy towels in a particular color *just* for that person.

- Buy washcloths and hand towels printed with pictures of your child's favorite storybook characters.

- Place press-on hooks at your child's level, so towels can be hung up more easily.

- Use a shower curtain ring to attach a hand towel to a towel bar. The towel will hang securely for hand drying.

Cutting Nails

- Cut an infant's nails at nursing time. Prop your baby's head on a pillow so you have both hands free.

- Use baby scissors with rounded tips. Or try a nail clipper; some say it's easier to use than baby scissors. (Keep one on your key ring.)

- Put baby powder in your palm and scrape your child's nails over it. Enough will stick under the nails to show you how far to cut without hurting your baby.

- Cut your baby's nails while she's sleeping. Or cut them after a meal when she's sleepy and content.

- Turn on a children's video or television show to keep an older child distracted.

- Trim your child's nails after a bath when they're soft and easy to cut.

- Try filing a child's nails instead.

- Clean under little nails with a flat wooden toothpick.

- Protect an active baby from self-scratching by putting tiny, lightweight crew socks over both hands. Some sleepers and gowns come with mitts, but many do not.

Cutting Hair

Keep in mind that time is of the essence when cutting hair. Use sharp shears. The job will go faster. What can't be done in five minutes probably won't get done. Keep your child occupied by talking and letting him watch what's going on in a mirror. Make it clear that haircutting is a job for *adults only*. If your pre-schooler abides by this rule, you'll be lucky!

• Wait until your little one is tired and falls asleep in the high-chair. Then work your magic. Results may not be high style, but the bulk of it will be off without a scene.

• Call a haircut a "trim." *Cuts hurt!* Talk about "fixing" or "making hair pretty."

• Place your child in a highchair or on a stool outdoors. Spread newspaper to catch falling hair. (Hair doesn't disintegrate as yard clippings do.)

• Wrap your child in a large beach towel or small sheet to keep hair from falling inside clothes and causing itchiness.

• Let your child wear a Halloween mask or swim goggles to keep hair out of his eyes.

• Cut your child's hair with electric hair clippers. (They tickle!)

• Provide your child with a squirt bottle (like the stylist uses) to spray water on his hair. Or spray a comb with water and run it through your child's hair. (Hair is easier to cut when it's wet.)

• Use a visor when trimming bangs, so hair falls away from your child's face. Remember that wet hair bounces up when it dries, so allow an extra quarter- or half-inch.

• Place a piece of paper or cardboard between your child's hair and forehead to keep hair snips and scissors away from your child's face.

- Trying to cut bangs straight? Dampen your child's hair with a little water or conditioner. Imagine a line drawn from outer eyebrow to outer eyebrow. Use a comb to hold your child's hair in place while you trim across. Or hold your child's chin to keep his head steady.

- Put a piece of transparent tape (or special hair tape that pulls off easily) across your child's bangs, and cut evenly above it.

- Don't cut bangs all the way to the sides. Cut just the center area and it will look better.

- Keep a child quiet by letting him play with something that's usually forbidden (costume jewelry, a deck of cards, and so on). Or give your child a special treat. Suckers can be time consuming!

- Play beauty parlor. For girls, a reward for sitting still can be having one's nails polished. (Even boys like clear polish.)

- Strap your toddler into a car seat on a kitchen table, and turn on a favorite television show or video.

- Cut hair in the bathtub while your child is busy playing and the hair is already wet.

- Make sure to have a mirror handy so your child can admire the effect.

- End the haircut on a high note with a few drops of cologne or perfume.

- Spray a tissue with hair spray, and use it to pick up tiny hair clippings.

The Unkindest Cut of All

Few children get through childhood without at least one incident of self-barbering. A quick trip to an understanding professional should repair or disguise the damage.

The More Costly Cut

When home haircutting becomes a bigger hassle than it's worth, it's time to go to a barber or hair stylist. Consider one who specializes in children's hair, at least for the first time or two. The environment is usually less intimidating, and it sets a pleasant tone for future haircuts.

• Prepare your child for a professional haircut by letting your little one accompany you to a salon the next time you get a haircut. Watching you or a sibling get a haircut should make your child feel more comfortable with the idea. Remember to take your child only after nap or mealtime.

• Take two children of similar ages to get simultaneous cuts. They'll watch each other and compete to see who's more "grown-up."

• Give your child a shampoo before going for a haircut. Or wet hair before arriving if shampooing at the salon is a hassle.

• Let your child sit on your lap with capes covering both of you if your child refuses to sit in the chair alone.

• Let your child play with the hair clips and cape as a distraction.

Dental Care

Diet is the first line of defense against dental problems. Between-meal snacks and highly sugared foods contribute to tooth decay. Frequent brushings remove the plaque that leads to decay. Brushing after snacks, even healthful ones like raisins or fruit juice, is particularly important. Toddlers and preschoolers, however enthusiastic, need help with toothbrushing. The manual dexterity needed to thoroughly clean every surface of every tooth doesn't develop until the age of six or seven. To show your child where plaque collects on teeth and where decay can start, put a drop of food coloring on a cotton swab, and rub it around your child's teeth and gums. The remaining stains will indicate where to clean.

Pediatric dentists recommend that your child's routine dental exams should begin sometime between six months and a year (when two or three teeth are in). The American Academy of Pediatrics believes age three is early enough, unless there are signs of a problem. Some parents take their children to their regular family dentists; others prefer pediatric dentists (pedodontists) who are specially trained to deal with the anxieties and emotions of youngsters. It's as important for a dentist to watch the shape of the child's mouth and to check the child's bite as it is to check for cavities.

Toothbrushing Routines

- Consider cleaning your baby's first tooth or two with a small gauze pad dipped in water. Rub the pad over the teeth and gums very gently to remove plaque and food debris. You may want to lay your baby on your lap. If you encounter resistance, cuddle your baby on your lap and make a game of rubbing and massaging his teeth with your clean finger. Eventually move to a small, wet washcloth, and after a while introduce a baby toothbrush.

- Lay a cooperative child down on a bed or your knees to have better access to new little teeth.

- Let an older child practice brushing in the tub, where one can splatter, drool, and gargle to one's heart's content.

- Have well water tested for fluoride. If levels are too low, your doctor may prescribe fluoride drops.

- Get little mouths to open wide for brushing by having them make noises. "Hee Hee" and "Ha Ha" will allow plenty of room. A Tarzan yell is also effective. Or ask your child if you can "find" monsters, relatives, and cartoon characters deep inside his mouth.

- Shield your eyes from the "dazzling shine" of teeth well brushed!

- Run toothbrushes through the dishwasher periodically to keep them germ free. Place them in the silverware basket.

- Hold off on the toothpaste until your child is two or three, since children can't spit it out until then. If you want to use a little toothpaste earlier, dab only a small amount on the baby toothbrush. Swallowing too much fluoride is not good for a child.

- Place toothpaste on your child's toothbrush and leave it on the sink. That way you'll know if your child brushed without asking.

Maximum Efficiency

- Get your child to brush longer (and understand the purpose of it) by naming every food your child has eaten that day. Brush each food away one at a time.

- Prolong the process by seeing how many faces you can make while brushing your teeth together. Keep score while you both continue to brush.

- Use an egg timer. The brushing continues until the sand is down. Or use a kitchen timer, music box, or recorded song.

Helpful Aids

- Let children use an electric toothbrush if they like the vibration. The cordless kinds are easiest to handle.

- Offer a selection of toothbrushes and toothpastes in a variety of colors and flavors. Sample sizes and travel sizes work well. (You may find that mint-flavored toothpastes are too strong for your child's sensitive taste buds.) A fruit-flavored one may be fun.

- Tape over half of the hole in a toothbrush holder so your child's smaller toothbrush doesn't fall through.

Tooth Fairy Fun

- Get across early the idea that the tooth fairy pays a whole lot more for a perfect tooth than for a decayed one. In some families, the tooth fairy leaves both a payment and a note praising the child for good dental habits.

- Sprinkle or spray glitter on the coins brought by the tooth fairy.

- Have the tooth fairy lead your child on a treasure hunt to find the reward. The first clue should be left where your child left his tooth.

- Tell your child that the tooth fairy's wings must be wet in order for her to fly and make nightly rounds. Your child should leave a glass of water on the windowsill or nightstand. The next morning the water will have mysteriously changed color from the magic dust that washed off the tooth fairy's wings. (Add food coloring, gelatin, or glitter.)

• Have the tooth fairy leave a note in tiny handwriting praising your child for a job well done. Use a paper doily for added fun.

• Have your child place the tooth in a small, sealed envelope under the pillow. The tooth fairy exchanges this envelope for a similar one containing coins or cash and an encouraging note.

Toilet Training

While you may wish to choose the time to toilet train your child (spring and summer are the most convenient seasons), be aware that no child will be trained until physically and emotionally ready (from eighteen to thirty months, or even older). Some of the signs of readiness include dry diapers for a couple hours at a time, the ability to understand simple commands and explanations, a desire to mimic adults' bathroom routines, an inclination toward tidiness, and a dislike of being wet or soiled.

Remember that if you try to push things, you'll only be training yourself to catch your child. If your child is not responding or showing an interest, or if you find yourself in a battle of wills, put the whole thing off for a few weeks or months. Relax, and don't pay too much attention to friends' and relatives' advice. By the time your child goes to school, you'll wonder why toilet training seemed like such a big deal.

Basic Training

Once basic training is underway, help your child understand that toilet habits are his or her own responsibility, including cleanups after accidents. Make it clear that this is not a punishment, just a matter of taking care of oneself.

• Put the potty chair (if you opt for one) in the bathroom a few months before you think your child will be ready to use it. Explain that when your child is old enough, it will be there to use. It's okay for your child to sit on it with clothes on to get used to it.

- Try letting your child go without bottom clothing altogether when training starts. (You'll have to be a bit brave to do this, or at least be a good observer and willing to do an occasional cleanup. Even carpet cleaning may be worth the investment if it does the trick.)

- Make potty cleaning easier by putting an inch or so of water or several sheets of toilet tissue in the bottom of the pot before each use. (Don't use bleach. Urine contains ammonia that will cause a dangerous chemical reaction.)

- Let your child learn by watching you or an older child use the toilet.

- Help your child learn what's expected by reading potty books like *KoKo Bear's New Potty* (Book Peddlers, 800–255–3379). There are lots of potty books available that help children understand what to expect and what's expected.

- Keep a box of flushable baby wipes in the bathroom for your child to use instead of toilet paper. They're easy for kids to use and help cut down on wasted toilet paper.

- Bring along a potty chair or use an inflatable one when traveling, so you can stop along the road instead of having to worry about finding a gas station. Line it with a plastic bag ahead of time. A little boy can do his business nicely in an empty coffee can lined with a plastic bag. Fill the bag partway with toilet tissue, paper towels, or even a disposable diaper to avoid sloshing.

- Keep a basket of children's books by the potty to keep a child sitting longer, or sing songs with your child.

Rewards (a.k.a. Behavior Modification)

No, you're not setting yourself up for a lifetime of rewarding correct toileting behavior. But it has helped many kids on the road to dryness.

- Buy "big boy" or "big girl" underpants as an incentive for training. At the very least move away from disposables once training has begun. Disposables don't allow children to feel wet and uncomfortable. (You can put a disposable pull-up diaper *over* cloth panties for household protection.)

- Keep a supply of small wrapped toys in a clear container where they can be easily seen. Or keep a supply of M&Ms on hand.

- Have your child call grandparents or other relatives to relate the good "potty" news.

- Buy a special book or toy after a week of dry pants.

- Use a progress chart with stars or other stickers to mark the days or parts of days without accidents. Place it in the bathroom or on the refrigerator door. (Print out a free progress chart at www.practicalparenting.com/pottyprogresschart.html.) When your child has mastered this stage of development, make your own potty diploma (or print one out at www.practicalparenting.com/pottydiploma.html), and fill in your child's name.

Using the Big Toilet

Some children are afraid of the big toilet. Help your child overcome these fears by explaining the body waste process and by showing your child the sewer pipes and other plumbing involved in waste removal.

- Let a child who's training on a potty chair use the big toilet occasionally. It will be easier to use when you're away from home.

- Teach a little girl to sit backward on the big toilet (some boys even like this position) or to perch on it sideways.

- Turn on the faucet and let the water run to help "inspire" your child.

93

- Float a piece of tissue or a Cheerio in the toilet to provide a target when teaching a boy to aim.

- Squirt some shampoo in the toilet so your child can make bubbles while urinating.

- Supply a sturdy footstool to help your child feel more secure and to help a young boy stand tall enough for the big toilet. A step stool is an important addition to any bathroom to help ensure that a child's hands get washed after using the toilet or potty seat.

Bedwetting

Nighttime wetting, which can continue into the preschool years and beyond (more often for boys than girls) is frustrating for children and parents alike. It's wise to check with your doctor to make sure there are no underlying physical causes. A recent report indicates that bedwetting can be related to an allergic response to cow's milk. Or it can simply mean that the child is sleeping soundly and not reading the body's signals.

Don't feel like you have to wait it out. Diet, behavior modification, and positive imaging are successful methods to explore. Bedwetting is not a psychological problem, but it is a laundry problem.

- Use a zippered plastic cover to protect your child's mattress (and pillow, if necessary). Or use a mattress pad with the plastic side down.

- Place a large towel between the mattress pad and sheet so you'll need to change only the towel and sheet. Or use a waterproof crib pad, an old plastic tablecloth, an inexpensive shower curtain (cut to size), or a large plastic garbage bag (slit into one large piece) between the sheet and the mattress pad. Even a rubber-backed bath rug can do the job.

- Keep two sets of bedding (including waterproof pads) on your child's bed, so you only have to remove the soiled set in the middle of the night.

- Buy large, rubber-backed flannel pads in a fabric store if they're not available in a juvenile department.

- Consider waking your child during the night for a trip to the toilet. This won't cure bedwetting, but it may prevent a wet bed. You may want to use an alarm clock.

- Reduce fluids during the late afternoon and evening hours.

- Double-diaper your child if you're still using diapers. For a larger child, buy large or youth-size diapers from a local medical supply company. For an up-to-date list of companies providing large cloth and disposable diapers and underpads, and for a complete discussion of toilet training, check my book *Toilet Training: A Practical Guide to Daytime and Nighttime Training* (Book Peddlers, 800–255–3379).

- Assure your child that bedwetting will be outgrown eventually (as long as there is no physical cause).

First Aid

Even the most carefully reared and watched child will sometimes get hurt or sick. Knowing how to handle minor accidents gives parents a sense of control. A good first-aid booklet and a book or two on home medical care are recommended. (The first-aid booklet belongs in a place where you can find it in a hurry. Protect its cover with clear Contact paper.)

Remaining calm in a crisis will help your child remain calm. Remember that a good venting cry may be the best thing for a hurt child. When you think your child has cried long enough, say so. Teach your child that feelings should be expressed, but there's also a time to regain control.

Handling Owies

Many of life's little owies can be cured by kissing the hurt area, by gently blowing on it, or by running it under warm or cold water. Some owies are a bit more painful and need more creativity and patience.

Cleaning a cut or scrape may be easier by bathing the child in a tub rather than focusing on the sore spot. Hydrogen peroxide is good for cleaning bloody scrapes as well as bloodstains on clothes.

- Make pain time applause time. The whole family can gather to praise bravery under difficult conditions.

- Use a red or other dark-colored washcloth to clean a bloody wound. The blood won't show, and your child will be less scared. (You can always store a dry one in a plastic bag in the freezer so you'll know where to find it.) Likewise, keep red paper napkins on hand to blot blood before you wash.

- Pin an "Ouch" sign on your child's clothes over a sensitive or hurt area, to alert playmates and siblings to be careful. (But be aware that kids older than four or five may find it fun to hit right there!)

- Paint a funny face or animal on the sore area.

- Help your child stop crying by asking her to whistle. It's impossible to cry and whistle at the same time.

- Distract and minimize the discomfort of getting a shot by bringing along a paper party blower for your child to play with. Or have your child repeatedly blow out of her mouth (as though blowing bubbles) while the shot is being given.

- Supply a "pain bell" for your child to ring, or a whistle to blow on until treatment has been completed.

- Have your child count while a shot is being given, to "see how long it takes."

- Coach your child in relaxation and breathing techniques of prepared childbirth methods. Breathe in time together!

Bumps and Bruises

Heat or cold? Which should you use to keep swelling down and speed healing? Cold will help numb the pain and stop the bleeding that causes black and blue marks under the skin, but use it for only twenty-four hours after a bruise occurs. After that, heat applied five or six times a day for a few days will speed recovery. Moderation is the key. Use nothing too hot or too cold. Don't apply ice cubes directly to tender skin. (Wrap them in a washcloth.) And don't use a high setting on a heating pad.

- Keep a supply of Popsicles in the freezer for pleasurable treatment of a bumped lip.

- Try putting the inside of a piece of banana skin on a bruise, and covering it with a cool, wet cloth to prevent excessive discoloration. (This is especially effective in preventing a black eye, and far less expensive than the traditional beefsteak!)

- Prepare ready-made cold compresses by freezing wet washcloths or leak-proof, self-closing freezer bags filled with water.

- Use a bag of frozen peas or a bag of frozen, uncooked rice for a flexible cold compress. Or fill a zip-lock bag with rubbing alcohol and water (diluted 1:3) for a compress that won't freeze solid.

- Use a can of frozen juice concentrate for a quick, nondrip compress.

- Freeze several small water-filled balloons that can be wrapped in a paper towel and applied to bumps. Add a little rubbing alcohol to the water before freezing, so they'll mold to "fit."

- Make a handy ice pack by folding a paper towel into a three-by-five-inch rectangle. Moisten the paper towel and freeze it in a zip-lock sandwich bag.

- Keep your child's old teething rings in the freezer to use as mini ice packs.

- Keep a packet of salad dressing or soy sauce in the freezer to put on bumps and bruises. They're perfect for little hands.

- Chill a hard-boiled egg in the refrigerator (or put it in the freezer for a few minutes) to use as a cold compress for a bruised eye.

- Fill empty plastic medicine bottles with water, seal them with childproof caps, and freeze. Use as needed for bumps or minor burns.

- Heat up a batch of damp washcloths in a crockpot for a steady supply of hot compresses.

- Microwave several small, rolled-up damp cloths in a plastic bowl for about a minute. Reheat as needed.

- Place a small, inflated swimming tube around the waist of a baby who's just learning to sit up without assistance, to cushion sideways falls.

Bandaging

Probably no item in your medicine chest is as magical in its healing powers as a single adhesive Band-Aid. And if one is good, several are even better. Plain ones, colorful ones, or those you decorate yourself all work wonders!

- Offer your child a Band-Aid the next time he complains of a stomachache. It will help localize the hurt, which may be all that's needed to cure it.

- Let your child put a Band-Aid on the same ouch spot on a doll, so the pain can be shared and lessened.

- Draw a star or heart on a Band-Aid to improve its healing power.

- Cover a scraped knee or elbow with the cutoff top of an old sock, to give extra protection to the Band-Aid underneath while allowing for movement. Or use a terry cloth wristband.

- Use a Popsicle stick to make a finger splint, or slip a small plastic hair roller over the injured finger to protect it from painful knocks.

- Make a square Band-Aid fit better over a fingertip or toe by making a diagonal cut at each corner as far in as the gauze pad. Wrap the Band-Aid around the fingertip or toe for a snug fit.

- Put transparent tape over a Band-Aid to hold it in place longer. Transparent tape and a piece of gauze make an excellent bandage when you don't have a regular Band-Aid available.

- Put medicine on the gauze pad (not the sore) when it's necessary to apply something that stings.

- Saturate a piece of cotton with baby oil, and rub it over the adhesive parts of a Band-Aid for easy removal. Or soften the adhesive parts by using a hair dryer set on warm.

- Wait until tub time to remove a Band-Aid. Let it soften under water, and have your child apply some soap if necessary. Removing it underwater may work best.

Splinters

- Get your supplies arranged beforehand: a bright light, tweezers or a sterile needle, and a magnifying glass (if necessary). Sterilize the needle by holding it in a flame or in boiling water for a few seconds.

- Prepare the splinter by soaking the area in warm water or olive oil, by covering it with a wet bandage or a piece of adhesive tape for a few hours, or by holding it over steam.

- Soak a finger in warm water with antibacterial soap. Once the skin is softened, it will be easier to remove the splinter.

- Paint hard-to-find splinters with Merthiolate or iodine. They'll show up as dark slivers.

- Numb the splinter area with ice or a little teething lotion.

- Ask your child to look the other way and sing a song, count, or recite something while you gently prod at the splinter with a sterile needle.

- Remove a metal splinter easily and painlessly with a magnet.

- Use tweezers to remove any large pieces. If small pieces remain, apply a household glue (such as Elmer's) with a cotton swab to the splinter area. Cover with gauze and let dry. When dry, remove the gauze and glue together. The remaining pieces should come out. (Good with cactus needles.)

- If you can't get a splinter out, let well enough alone. Most splinters eventually work themselves to the surface. (For one that doesn't, you may want to see your doctor.)

Your Child Has a Bug in Her Ear?

Take your child into a dark room and shine a flashlight near her ear. Many bugs will be attracted to the light and crawl out. If that doesn't work, drip a few drops of rubbing alcohol into the ear to kill the bug. (The alcohol may sting if there's a scratch inside the ear.) Have your child turn her head so the ear is facing down, and shake her head. The bug should drop out. Never try to get hold of a bug with tweezers or other instruments. You might push the bug farther in, and there's a chance you could rupture your child's eardrum.

Bites and Stings

In addition to the host of commercial products available for treating bites and stings, many simple household remedies work well.

- Rub a bar of wet soap over the bite, or apply toothpaste to it.

- Apply a paste of water and meat tenderizer.

- A paste of baking soda and water applied *immediately* to a bee or wasp sting also reduces pain and swelling.

- Cut off the tip of an aloe plant and apply the sap to the bite. Or buy aloe gel at a health food store. (It's also good for sunburn.)

- Hold a piece of ice wrapped in a cloth on the sting area until it's numbed.

- Crisscross the swollen area around a mosquito bite with a fingernail (on the theory that one pain will cancel another), and apply some ever-available spit.

- Let an itchy child soak in a tub of water containing baking soda or laundry starch. Or go to the beach just for the sake of getting in the soothing water!

• Neutralize the sting of fire ants by applying white vinegar to the bites.

In Sickness and in Health

We experienced our parents' care when we were sick as children, but the job of caring for our own sick children seems awesome. As parents we act as paramedics, comforters, and companions to our sick children. Until your children can *tell* you what's bothering them, these roles can be especially difficult. Many of the tips in the Doctor Visits section (pages 33–35) apply to the care of toddlers and preschoolers as well as infants.

Taking Temperatures

Digital thermometers have made this job much faster and easier for parents. Glass thermometers are no longer recommended because of the risk of mercury poisoning if the glass breaks. The rectal temperature is the most accurate. It will be one degree higher than an oral temperature.

Other methods will give you a "ballpark" temperature if you simply want an indication as to whether your child is running a fever. One is to kiss your child's forehead. (The temperature of your lips is more stable than that of your hands.) Other options include axillary (armpit) thermometers, the ear thermometer (not recommended in children under three months), and the forehead strip. It's important to tell your doctor which method you used when you report a temperature.

• Make insertion of a rectal thermometer easier by smearing petroleum jelly on it.

• Give your child an egg timer or kitchen timer to watch while her temperature is being taken. Or let your child watch TV or listen to a song, or sing one together to shorten the wait.

• Don't take your child's temperature immediately after a bath; this can affect the temperature reading.

Giving Medication

One of the hardest things about giving medicine to babies and small children is getting it all down. Don't try putting it in a bottle of formula or juice; you won't know how much your baby has received if all the liquid isn't taken.

- Give your baby liquid medicine in a nipple. (Make sure all the medication is taken by filling the nipple with a little water for your child to suck.) Or use an eyedropper, vitamin dropper, or medicine syringe (without the needle), which you can buy at the drugstore. Squirting into the cheek area (not down the throat) is easy, there's no mess, and 5 milliliters (ml) equal one teaspoon.

- Give bad-tasting medicine by holding your child's nose until the medicine is swallowed. Then give some gum or a drink while continuing to hold your child's nose.

- Many of today's good-tasting medicines can be frozen as Popsicles, but check with your doctor first!

- Ask your physician for the more concentrated medicine. Many antibiotics come in two strengths: 125 milligrams (mg) per 5 ml (or one teaspoon), and 250 mg per 5 ml. If the dose is 250 mg, you only have to get your child to swallow half a teaspoon of the more concentrated medicine instead of a whole teaspoon of the less concentrated type.

- Chilling liquid medicines can improve the flavor.

- Call medicine "the slime" or some other humorous name. Most medicines these days are quite tasty, which actually causes safety problems because a child may wish to take more when you're not around.

- Use a hollow, graduated medicine spoon for giving medicine to older children. Check your drugstore or talk to your pharmacist.

- Hold a paper cup under your child's chin when giving liquid medicine. Spills can be mixed with water or fruit juice and drunk from the cup.

- Taste the medicine yourself, and tell your child if it tastes bad. If it does, rub an ice cube over your child's tongue to numb the taste buds.

- Wrap a small child in a bath towel to limit physical resistance.

- If your child absolutely refuses medicine by clamping his jaws shut, gently squeeze his nostrils shut. His mouth will open quickly!

- An older child may enjoy watching the procedure in a mirror.

A No-No

Never give aspirin to babies or young children unless your doctor instructs you to do so. Instead, use acetaminophen (such as Liquid Tylenol) in weight-appropriate doses to treat your child's fever. Talk to your doctor before giving your child any medication. Check the package for recommended doses.

Pill Skills and Drills

- Butter a pill lightly or coat it with salad oil to help it go down easily. Or bury it in a spoonful of applesauce.

- Let an older child hold a marshmallow to eat *after* the medicine is taken.

- Place a pill in a teaspoonful of ice cream or whipped cream, and it will slide down.

- Press a pill between two spoons to crush it, then mix it with applesauce and jam. Serve it by spoon with a "chaser" of water or juice.

- "Give" the pill to your child's favorite stuffed animal first. Or give it during a bath or when your child is distracted with toys.

- Place a pill on your child's tongue, and have him take two gulps of water or juice in quick succession from a narrow-neck bottle. The pill should go down with the second gulp.

- Ask your pharmacist for an empty, labeled bottle for your child's medicine. Put your child's daytime medicine in the bottle and give it to your daycare provider.

- Jot down the time, amount, and medicine given if you have more than one medication to administer to your child, or if you have more than one child taking more than one medicine. Keep the dosage sheet posted on the refrigerator. Memory can fail anyone—and often does!

- Hang a card on the refrigerator that shows the doses and days. Cross off each dose as you go along to ensure that you give the proper number of doses.

- Let your doctor know if your child has not improved within forty-eight hours of taking medicine.

Constipation

Children's bowel movement patterns vary as much as their height and weight. Constipation (defined by hardness, not frequency) is best treated by dietary changes. Give your constipated child lots of water and fruit juice (yes, prune juice), high-fiber foods such as bran cereal and graham crackers (not soda crackers), and dried fruits for snacks. Avoid binding foods such as apples, bananas, rice, and gelatin. Decrease milk products for a few days. Other mild laxatives you can use sparingly include a spoonful of honey (in children older than one year), a bit of milk of magnesia, or a little mineral oil camouflaged in something else. Call your doctor if your child experiences great pain passing stools or if blood appears in stools.

- Spread a little petroleum jelly on your child's rectum or on a thermometer inserted into your child's rectum.

- Sit in the bathroom with your child. Little bottoms don't fit comfortably on adult toilet seats, and moral and physical support helps.

- Help your child hold her "cheeks" open to make passage easier.

Diarrhea

As with constipation, mild diarrhea is often treated with dietary changes. Binding foods such as bananas, rice, applesauce, and pasta often help. However, diarrhea can be caused by a number of serious illnesses or allergies. If your child has loose, watery stools for more than a day, call your doctor. The threat of dehydration is very serious. If your child is listless and lethargic and unable to retain fluids, he may be dehydrated. Other symptoms include low urine output, dry mouth, few tears during crying, sunken eyes, and dry skin. Test for dehydration by pinching a small fold of skin on the back of your child's hand. If it fails to sink back down when released, your child may be dehydrated.

- Encourage an infant with diarrhea to continue breastfeeding, or offer rehydration fluids such as Pedialyte. Avoid sports drinks and sugary beverages.

- If your child is having a hard time accepting liquids, try giving them in a tiny glass such as a shot glass.

- Serve liquids in a fancy adult glass to make drinking more appealing, but avoid lead crystal.

- Try weird-shaped straws to make drinking more interesting.

- Give Jell-O water. This homemade binder is made by dissolving a three-ounce package of Jell-O in a cup of cold tap water.

- Try water in which rice has been cooked; it's a binder, too.

- Don't give a commercial binding product to a child under five or six without consulting your doctor.

Calling the Doctor

Put your crying baby down before calling the doctor, or have someone else hold your baby; otherwise, neither you nor the doctor will be able to hear very well.

The Heave-Ho's

- Give ice chips instead of water to a child who can't keep liquids down. A child shouldn't drink liquids after vomiting, but ice chips will help remove the bad taste.

- Place a plastic wastebasket on the floor next to your child's bed, or keep a plastic mixing bowl and bath towel near the bedside.

- Spread towels over your child's pillow and blanket. They're easier to remove and launder than bed linens.

- Cover vomit immediately with cat litter or baking soda to minimize odors and facilitate cleanup.

Colds and Flus

- Help prevent colds during the cold-and-flu season by putting all the toothbrushes in the dishwasher every few days.

- Wash hands frequently to prevent and combat illnesses during the cold-and-flu season.

- Teach your children how to blow their nose by having them close their mouth and pretend to blow out a candle with their nose.

- Use an old, soft washcloth or a soft handkerchief to wipe a tender nose. Or use tissues with lotion.

- Use an electric coffee maker (with the lid removed) as a steamer or vaporizer if a regular one isn't available. Make sure to place it where it can't be tipped over.

- Help relieve your child's congestion by running very hot water in the shower. Sit with your child in the bathroom with the door closed. (Some people recommend cold water shower "steam" for croup.)

- Hang a wet towel or sheet near a heat source to increase the humidity in a room and make labored breathing easier.

- Put a feverish child in a lukewarm tub and let him blow bubbles. When the child gets bored, give him a Popsicle. It's fun, there's no mess, and the fever comes down.

- Coat a sore nose with nonmentholated lip balm or petroleum jelly. Or put a little petroleum jelly on a tissue before wiping your child's nose.

Chicken Pox

- Give bored kids with chicken pox some paintbrushes and calamine lotion, and let them paint the pox marks. It will take them a while to do and will keep them from scratching. Calamine lotion covers quickly and dries fast.

- Quell the itch of chicken pox and other nuisances by using spray starch on the spots. (Make sure it doesn't contain sizing.)

- Put a little baking soda or Aveeno Oatmeal Bath in your child's tub.

Coughs and Sore Throats

- Use a pillow or folded blanket to elevate the head of the mattress to make breathing easier for a child with croup, congestion, or a bad cough. Or place a few books under the bed legs near your child's head.

- Make a cough medicine by mixing lemon juice and honey in equal parts. (Don't give honey to babies under one year of age; it may contain botulism spores that can cause infant botulism.)

- Teach your child to gargle by doing it yourself while singing a song; let your child join in.

Ear Infections

- Reduce or eliminate your child's intake of dairy products to help reduce the mucus that contributes to ear infections.

- Elevate the head of the mattress to help drain fluid.

- Prepare a child who will be having ear tubes inserted by reading *Koko Bear's Big Earache* (Book Peddlers, 800–255–3379).

Sickroom Logistics

- Avoid having to run from room to room by keeping medications and other sickroom supplies in a container such as a shoebox, basket, or bread pan.

- Use a lazy Susan for easy access to bedside supplies.

- Anchor a shoe bag between the bed mattress and frame. The pockets (hanging down over the edge) will hold tissue and other small necessities.

- Pin a paper bag to the side of the mattress for soiled tissues and other scraps.

- Make a table over your child's bed by using an adjustable ironing board, a card table with two legs folded up, or a big cardboard box cut to fit over your child's legs.

- Let a sick child lie on an adjustable chaise lounge from your outdoor furniture set. It allows for a variety of positions and eliminates continual propping.

- Use a parent's old T-shirt as a sick gown for a child with chicken pox, poison ivy, or some other skin problem requiring lotion. The shirt won't bind, and the lotion won't stain bedding or furniture.

- Serve tray meals with a damp washcloth or paper towel under the dishes to prevent them from slipping. The towel can be used to clean the patient's hands after eating.

• Cover the top blanket on your child's bed with a sheet that can be changed if food or liquid is spilled on it.

Casts on Arms and Legs

• Keep a leg or arm cast dry for showering or bathing by covering it with a large plastic bag held in place with a rubber band or waterproof tape.

• Lubricate the edges of a cast with petroleum jelly to prevent chafed skin.

• Sprinkle baby powder at the opening of a cast, and blow it in with a hair dryer or vacuum cleaner (with airflow reversed) to relieve itching.

• Clean up a dirty white cast with white shoe polish.

• Make regular jeans and pants usable over a leg cast by inserting a long zipper in the inseam. When the cast comes off, the zipper can be removed and sewn up.

Chapter 4

Coping with Kids at Home

The better organized a household is, the smoother it usually runs. With children around, you have to cope with one situation at a time. There are, nevertheless, plenty of things you can do to make coping easier.

Childproofing Your Home

One of the best things you can do is get down on the floor and crawl where your baby crawls (or *will* crawl—you'll want to childproof *before* your child starts moving). Carefully examine everything within reach. You'll discover objects your baby can choke on, sharp edges on the undersides of furniture, and loads of things that might break off or fall over.

When you're visiting someone else's home, remember that childproofing (and child-watching!) is *your* responsibility. For a more detailed discussion, read *Baby Proofing Basics* (Book Peddlers, 800–255–3379), but these tips will get you started.

The Kitchen Stove

• Turn all saucepan handles to the rear of the stove.

• Turn on the oven light when the oven's in use, and teach children that "Light on means hands off." Leave the light on until the oven is cool.

- Remove stove knobs, if you can, or tape them so children can't turn them. Or use stove knob covers.

- Lock the oven, fridge, and freezer doors with plastic latches that attach with adhesive.

- Back a high-back chair up to the stove for a young cook, and let your child stand or kneel on it. The chair back provides a barrier. (You're *right there,* of course.)

- Let an older child stir food on the stove with a long-handled wooden spoon. (Wood doesn't conduct heat.)

- Set a timer when you're cooking with kids around. Children are distracting, and you can easily ruin your food or cause a fire.

Around the Kitchen

- Use safety locks on drawers and cupboards. Several brands are available in hardware stores.

- Run a yardstick through suitable drawers and cabinet handles, or use metal shower rings or blanket clips to hold them shut.

- Secure cabinets with bungee cords, pieces of rope, or even a dog collar.

- Use wet paper towels or paper napkins to pick up small pieces of broken glass the broom doesn't get, so young crawlers won't cut their hands and knees.

- Let your child use plastic or paper cups instead of breakable glasses and china mugs. Store plastic cups in a drawer rather than a cupboard, so a child who's able to reach the faucet with a stool will be able to reach them.

- Attach a paper cup holder to the side of your refrigerator so kids won't keep using new glasses.

- Move all cleaning supplies out from under the sink, and lock them up. (Replace them with plastic containers and pans your kids can play with). If you don't use Mr. Yuk stickers, paint the caps of dangerous materials with red nail polish, and teach your children that red means danger.

- Beware of a child tasting detergent from the soap cup in the dishwasher. Add detergent only when you're ready to start the machine.

- Prevent smashed toes by putting shoes on a child who will be pulling cans or heavy objects from a kitchen cupboard.

- Don't use tablecloths until your child is past the grabbing stage.

The Bathroom

The bathroom poses an even greater risk of poisoning than the kitchen. Cleaning supplies and medicines must be locked up or put out of reach. A locking medicine chest is well worth the inconvenience. At the very least, create your own "lock" with strips of Velcro. Consider moving medicines and cleaning products to a high cupboard in the kitchen where they'll be safely out of reach.

While toilet tissue can't be considered dangerous, your child's "flushing fascination" period may cause waste and perhaps even pipe clogging. Many parents keep toilet tissue off the holder during this period or discourage waste by keeping a rubber band around the roll. It's possible to make a toilet tissue cover by cutting a five-inch center section from a plastic soda bottle, and cutting a two-inch-wide slit from top to bottom to fit over the roll. Or make the roll harder to spin by squeezing it so it's no longer round.

- Make sure grandparents take appropriate precautions with their medication bottles when kids are around.

- Replace childproof caps carefully and promptly after use. Save caps from empty bottles to use on other bottles or jars you want to childproof.

- Toilets, tubs, and diaper pails present drowning hazards. Children can drown in less than an inch of water. Drain water immediately after a bath, place safety latches on toilets, and keep diaper pails out of reach.

- Hang three-tiered wire mesh baskets in the bath or shower to keep shampoo, razors, and other dangerous items out of toddlers' hands.

- Take the phone off the hook, turn on your answering machine, or bring your cordless phone or cell phone in with you while you're bathing your child, so a ringing phone won't tempt you to leave your child alone in the tub.

Bathroom Door Safety

- Keep the bathroom off limits for a small child by securing a bolt or hook-and-eye screws high up on the outside of the door. Even a sock on a doorknob held in place with a rubber band will make it difficult for a child to open a closed bathroom door. Or use a plastic doorknob cover designed for this purpose.

- Drape a towel over the top of the bathroom door to keep a child from shutting it tightly and locking himself in. Or keep the door from closing completely by placing a large, ball-type ponytail holder over the upper and lower sections of the top hinge pin. Or tape the bathroom door latch flush with the side of the door to prevent lock-ins.

- Keep a key or tool outside the door to unlock it in an emergency.

- Remove the doorknob altogether if it doesn't unlock from the outside and you don't want to install one that does.

Your Child's Room

- Use a baby gate to keep your little one out of an off-limits room or private area, and later to protect your older child's room from a mobile infant or toddler.

- Check often for loose eyes on stuffed animals and for small toy parts that might break off. Throw out broken toys, for safety's sake.

- Store your child's clothes in open, stackable cubes or vegetable bins to enable easier access and to eliminate the possibility of your child pulling out a heavy drawer or toppling a bookcase on herself.

- Secure your child's bureau or heavy bookcase to the wall with hook-and-eye screws, to keep a climber from tipping them over.

- Avoid smashed fingers by gluing suction cups or small cork blocks on the underside corners of a toy chest lid. Or install a pneumatic door spring (like the one on a screen door) to make the lid open easily and close slowly. Better yet, store toys on open shelving.

- Don't place a crib or other climbable furniture near a window. Install window guards wherever needed.

- Remove labels from bibs and clothing to prevent your baby from chewing them off and choking. Even a baby with no teeth can remove them.

Graduating to the Big Bed

As a rule of thumb, a child thirty-five inches tall is big enough for a big bed.

- Let your toddler start to use a pillow while still in the crib. It helps children learn to center their body while asleep.

- Lower the side of the crib and put a stool beside it for a young walker who's about to graduate to a big bed. It's better to help your child climb out safely than risk a fall.

- Push one side of the big bed against the wall for a recent crib graduate, and put a crib mattress on the floor next to the open side to cushion an accidental fall. Or use a removable side rail on the open side for a few weeks.

- Start with a regular-size mattress or futon on the floor without a bed frame. You can even use the crib mattress for part of the transition.

- Turn your child's blanket crosswise, allowing for extra tuck-in along the mattress length.

- Roll up two blankets, and put one under each side of the mattress (lengthwise) to make a small "valley" for your child to sleep in. Or place one blanket under the open side of the mattress so it tilts slightly toward the wall.

- Fold crib sheets in half, trim off the edges, and stitch up the sides so your child can use the familiar sheets as pillowcases.

- Tuck the edges of the top sheet under the mattress to secure your child. A child can still wiggle out the top.

- Cover exposed metal areas with soft, thick pipe wrap (the kind used to insulate pipes). Metal bed frames can cause serious injury.

- Consider moving your child to a double bed instead of a twin bed. There's more room to cuddle at bedtime or when your child is sick. It also provides more sprawl room.

- Some parents like trundle beds. A child can sleep on the lower mattress pulled out at bedtime, or the lower mattress can cushion a fall from the higher mattress. They also give Mom or Dad a place to sleep when a child is sick or frightened.

If a Product Causes Injury

Contact the U.S. Consumer Product Safety Commission if you have any questions about the safety of a piece of equipment or furniture, or if you wish to report an incident or unsafe product. Call 800-638-2772; contact their website at www.cpsc.gov; or write to CPSC, Washington, DC 20207.

Doors and Windows

- Childproof windows with gratings or heavy screens. In some apartments you can use window brackets that allow windows to open only a few inches.

- Open windows from the top, if possible.

- Put decals at child's eye level on sliding glass doors as reminders that they are glass, not open space.

- Attach a bell to a door that a small child can open, to warn you if your child wanders out. Christmas ornament bells work well and look attractive.

- Fasten an old sock over the doorknob with a rubber band. Adult hands can squeeze hard enough to turn the knob; small hands can't.

- Put hook-and-eye screws high up on the outsides of doors to older children's rooms or other rooms you don't want toddlers to go into. (*Caution:* Children can be locked *in* by inattentive sitters or older siblings who are "just playing.") Use hook-and-eye screws to secure screen doors, too.

- Attach a flat curtain rod (at child's height) to a screen door you *want* your child to be able to push open, to keep your child from pushing out the screen.

- Keep tots from opening and closing sliding glass doors by placing a spring-loaded curtain rod between the outside frame and the sliding door.

Stairways

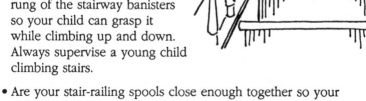

- Install a swinging gate at the top of the stairs. It can be secured when little ones are on the loose. A second gate at the bottom is also a good idea, to prevent young ones from climbing on stairs. (Never use a pressure gate at the top.)

- Teach toddlers to crawl downstairs backward ("toesies first") and to get down from furniture backward.

- Attach a rope to the lower rung of the stairway banisters so your child can grasp it while climbing up and down. Always supervise a young child climbing stairs.

- Are your stair-railing spools close enough together so your child can't fit through them? There are no standard safety regulations for railings.

Electricity

- Install childproof covers on every outlet in your home, and place furniture in front of outlets wherever possible. Replace baby-accessible covers with slide-locking ones, which are better than those that just plug in.

- Wind up excess lengths of electrical cords, and fasten them with rubber bands, twist ties, or cord shorteners to keep your child from sucking or chewing on them. Keep them behind furniture wherever possible.

- Buy childproof covers for power strips, or insert plugs into unused outlets on strips if you're using them for home computers or entertainment centers.

All Around Your Home

- Don't assume that squeezing books tightly into a bookcase will keep a determined toddler from pulling them out. Chances are the bookcase will topple before the child gives up.

- Leave lower bookshelves and the shelf under the television stand open for toys and children's books. Your possessions can be returned to their proper places in a few years.

- Keep small children and pets from playing in the soil around your indoor potted plants by buying an inexpensive roll of nylon screen from a hardware store. (Or use plastic mesh squares from craft stores.) Cut a circle the diameter of the top of the pot. Cut a slit to the center and slide the stem through. You can water through the screen.

- Install vinyl screen around lower bookshelves if you can't bear the thought of putting your books away. A screen will also discourage your toddler from climbing the shelves. Use Velcro and adhesives to fasten the screen to the adjacent wall or the sides of the bookshelves, so you can have access to the shelves.

- Wrap sheets of clear, durable plastic around anything you don't want your young child to get into or climb, such as a baker's rack or large floor plants. Tape or staple the sheet at the back.

- Cover the rods used for the handles and pedals of rocking horses (which can be hazardous if kids fall and bump against them) with rubber tips used for chair legs. Or use handlebar grips designed for bicycles.

- Turn a desk with its drawers to the wall. Use only the surface and eliminate the opportunity for the drawers to be opened and emptied.

- Pull chairs close to your dining table to discourage your toddler from climbing up on them.

- Put your baby in the infant seat *inside* the playpen when you must leave your baby and toddler alone together. Or put your toddler in the playpen!

- Put the Christmas tree inside a playpen to keep it out of your toddler's reach.

- Don't let your child run with a pencil, Popsicle stick, lollipop stick, or any similar object in her mouth. It's dangerous.

- *Never* leave a plastic bag (especially a dry-cleaning bag) where children can play with it over their head and suffocate. Get in the habit of knotting your plastic bags before throwing them away.

- Use pipe insulation to cover table legs that need to be protected. Slit the insulation, wrap it around the legs, and tape.

- Pad the corners of sharp tables with shoulder pads from your old outfits. Attach the pads securely with duct tape. (Tell friends it's the latest in shoulder-pad fashion!) Commercial products are also available for wrapping around the edges of sharp tables.

Preventing Accidental Poisoning

The most common causes of poisoning in children under six are drugs, plants, personal care products, and household cleaners. Monitor your children especially carefully before mealtimes—they're more liable to sample foreign substances when they're hungry. A bad smell or taste doesn't stop children from putting things in their mouths. Post the National Poison Control Center number (800-222-1222) near every phone in your home.

Teach your child to say, "Ahhh." You may get a chance to see what's in your child's mouth and pull it out before harm is done. Parents should also keep syrup of ipecac (available from pharmacies without a prescription) on hand to induce vomiting. But use it *only* if directed by the poison center or a doctor. Syrup of ipecac is sold in bottles containing two tablespoons; children under six are given only one tablespoon. The drug's shelf life is five years. Make sure to take a bottle with you when traveling.

Outdoor Safety

A whole new set of hazards presents itself to a child outdoors and away from home. There are attractive things to taste, unfamiliar settings to investigate, interesting equipment to experiment with, and dangerous streets to cross. There's also the possibility of getting lost.

You might consider attaching a trucker's side-view mirror to an appropriate spot outside your kitchen window, to keep a play area in your line of sight when your child first begins to play outside alone.

In the Yard

- Glue a rubber bathmat or attach nonslip bathtub strips to a swing seat to prevent your child from slipping off.

- Cover swing chains with sections of garden hose or pipe wrap foam to avoid torn clothes and to provide a more comfortable grip. Wrap adhesive or electrical tape around the hose or foam at the level of your child's grip.

- Spread four to six inches of loose material (such as sand or wood chips) under swings and other playground equipment, to cushion falls. Dirt can be very hard.

- Cover exposed screws and bolts with caps or tape. Use pliers to pinch the ends of S-hooks together so they can't snag your child's skin or clothing.

- Check your backyard equipment regularly to make sure it's safe, and check playground equipment at local parks.

- Place an extension ladder across the driveway a few feet from the end to keep preschoolers from riding trikes into the street. Or paint a red stripe across the driveway as a reminder.

Crossing Safely

For a child who doesn't want to hold your hand while crossing the street or parking lot, carry a doll or stuffed animal whose hand your child can hold while you hold the other hand of the toy. (Avoid this with a younger tot whose behavior is less predictable.)

In the Car

There is *no safe alternative* to an approved, reliable car restraint: a car seat for a baby or small child under 40 pounds, or a booster seat or seat belt for an older child. Parents who are tempted to transport a baby in an infant seat or portable crib or who let older children romp around in the back of a car are tempting fate. Plus, it's illegal. Children usually learn good safety habits if they're established from the start and *never* varied—and if parents and other adults set good examples by always buckling up. Protect your upholstery by putting a beach towel or car seat protector over your seats, and put a strip of heavy vinyl carpet runner under the car seat.

- Teach your children the following safety routine: "Hands up! Doors closed and locked! Belts fastened! Blast off!" An older child can be appointed "First Mate" to see that the procedure is carried out correctly.

- Pull over to the side of the road if there's screaming or fighting in the car. Stay there until everyone settles down.

- Spread a light-colored bassinet sheet, towel, or receiving blanket over a car seat in the summer to prevent a hot seat from burning your child's tender skin. When your child is old enough to use a seat belt, keep a towel in the car for the same purpose.

- Put a hat on a small child to shield her eyes from the sun. Or put solar film or a car shade on the window near the car seat.

- Transport sharp or heavy objects in the trunk or rear compartment, not in the passenger area.

- Never leave children unattended in a car, and never leave the motor running when children are playing near the car. Beware when backing up with children nearby.

Halloween Safety for the Very Young

This is probably *the* holiday high point of the year. Even little kids get into the spirit of it early on. It satisfies a need to dress up, pretend, and party—not to mention the thrill of getting candy. You can always limit your child's candy consumption (or make sure teeth are *really* well brushed), but don't let that get in the way of enjoying the holiday.

- Save money on Halloween treats by stamping your return address on baggies and filling them with different kinds of bulk candy. Parents will know the candy is safe, even if it's unwrapped.

- Make sure your children's costumes allow them to walk easily. Children should wear shoes that fit—not your high heels! And remember that face makeup is safer than a mask that may block vision at night. (Save such masks for daytime parties.) Make sure costume props (such as weapons) are made from flexible materials.

- Have your child carry a small container so it will look full faster and will be less cumbersome. Plastic bags, plastic pumpkin buckets, or even pillowcases work well.

- Put reflecting tape on costumes and containers your children will be carrying.

- Provide your child with a flashlight or light stick, even though you'll be nearby.

- Make sure your child understands that you must check treats before they're eaten. Feed your children before they leave, so they'll be less tempted to sample treats while trick-or-treating.

Getting Chores Done

B.C. (before children), when you could work without interruption, you may have had the best kept home in town. That's not possible with little kids around. "A clean home shows a life misspent" is a slogan you may wish to adopt. Lower your standards. Pick one or two rooms to keep neat and keep the kids out of them.

Keeping Kids Out of the Way

You can try to work "around" your kids, stopping when you must and pressing on when you can. Or you can let them "help" you. (Remember that sometimes they're really learning!) Or you can try to keep them out of the way by hiring a sitter, which is less expensive than hiring cleaning help and is a good way to check out a new sitter. The cardinal rule for many parents is "Naptime and bedtime are not signals for work to begin. They're for *private time!*"

- Put your baby in a padded laundry basket or small cardboard box with a few toys, so traveling from room to room with you is easy. It's a good way for your baby to practice sitting for short periods of time. Or keep your child in a stroller or playpen with wheels as you move from room to room.

- Let the parent who's not doing the housework entertain the child.

- Put your baby in a backpack or front pack. He'll be where he wants to be (near you), and your hands will be free to work.

- Place a child with limited mobility in an empty plastic molded swimming pool when you're doing chores outside.

- Swings, doorway bouncers, and exersaucers are alternatives to playpens.

- Keep track of your child while cooking dinner by taking the tray off the highchair and moving the chair to the grown-up table. Cut open grocery bags, tape them to the table as far as your child can reach, and provide crayons. You'll have time for some no-worry cooking.

- Assign your child his own kitchen drawer or cupboard stocked with assorted plastic containers, wooden spoons, and other safe kitchen items.

- Allow your child to play in water in the sink while you work in the kitchen, but do it on a day you plan to wash the floor! Always keep an eye on your child near water.

- Give a small child a wadded piece of cellophane or masking tape to play with *near you* if you want a few minutes of quiet time to work or talk on the phone. Or put a dab of baby lotion, peanut butter, or vegetable oil on the highchair tray to keep your child busy.

- Curb your child's impatience for the cake to be done or for playtime with you to begin by setting a timer and letting him watch it run down.

Encouraging Neatness

- Color-code your child's everyday belongings. Have your child use the blue toothbrush, blue towels and washcloths, blue drinking cup, and blue brush. Use a colored marker or colored stickers to color-code your child's other belongings.

- Keep a clean dustpan in the toy box so your child can scoop up small objects.

- Make cleaning a messy room easier for your kids by sweeping or raking toys into the center of the room so there's only one pile. Sometimes one mess is easier to deal with than scattered messes.

- Let anything you have to pick up simply "disappear" for a time.

- Offer to pick up your child's toys occasionally in return for your child doing one of your simpler chores. Or work along with your child; it's more fun to work together than alone.

- Encourage your child to pick up toys after an activity is finished instead of waiting until the end of the day when the task is overwhelming.

- Have your child help pick up before leaving a friend's house.

- Help your kids put their things in the right places on open shelving by drawing labels and taping them to the appropriate shelves.

- Install a basketball hoop over your kids' laundry hamper to provide an incentive for tossing in dirty clothes.

- Keep a tall, narrow plastic container in each child's closet for storing dirty clothes. Or hang a colorful pillowcase with loops sewn onto it on the back of your child's bedroom door.

- Have a child who gets an allowance pay you a penny for each toy or article of clothing you pick up and store in a big box or bag until payment is collected. Or have your child do a special chore for the return of a toy.

- Set a good example by putting your things away, too.

Kids Really Helping

Even small children can help around the house if you're patient and don't expect perfection. It's important to remember to stress the importance of *all* work, to express appreciation for any job well done, and to switch assignments occasionally to avoid boredom. If you're cheerful at your work and find humor in humdrum activities, your kids will probably follow suit. Rewards inspire help, too, and the "house fairy" may visit often to leave treats for good workers. Make it a rule *never* to redo work a child (or your partner!) has done. Willing help will be hard to come by if you do.

- Give your child a smiling-face sticker to put in a place where she has done an unasked chore or favor. Make sure to notice the sticker and praise your child.

- Print titles of jobs on slips of paper when there's a lot to do and you want everyone to pitch in. Include some that say "Hop on one foot" and "Eat one cookie." For little kids, draw pictures that illustrate such jobs as "Feed the dog" and "Set the table."

- Give your child a reason for cleaning up, and set a deadline such as "before Daddy comes home" or "by lunchtime." Not having to do it right away gives your child a choice, and having a deadline encourages getting it done in a timely manner.

- Let the child closest to the floor pick things up and give them to you or an older child to put away (when picking up is a group project).

- Sometimes giving kids a list of things you'd like done works better than nagging them. Or put a wheel chart on the refrigerator. Or post a "Help wanted" board with optional chores kids can do to earn more allowance (such as watering plants and organizing recycling materials).

Making Chores Fun

- Assign each child a specific number of items to pick up, and teach counting as the job gets done. Or have your child pick up items whose names begin with letters you call out (or that are the colors you name).

- Put pocket sponges on the feet of smaller kids who want to help mop the kitchen (but the mop is too big for them).

- Make dusting or polishing the car more fun by slipping old socks over kids' hands.

- Create a "Dust Monster" from an unmatched sock. Decorate it with markers, use felt circles for eyes, and let your little one help you clean with it. Or give your child a thick, soft-bristled paintbrush to "paint" the dust away.

- Make a game of setting the table by having one child be the waiter and the other child be the cleanup person. Switch every day.

- Encourage your child to dust or vacuum by placing pennies on the places that need cleaning up. Your child will pick up the coins while going about the task at hand.

- Put a time limit on chores by using a timer or by playing a song on the stereo. Or have a race to see who can finish a chore first, if the quality of the work isn't really important. Keep track of who does the most, and provide a reward such as being the first to take a turn at a board game.

Getting Organized

Most parents like to save time, money, and trouble. Finding a clever use for an item that's no longer needed for its original purpose, protecting a piece of furniture so it outlasts its expected lifetime, making a child's room a haven of comfort and convenience at little or no cost...all can give a feeling of accomplishment.

Something Out of Something Else

- Use your baby's outgrown plastic bathtub for water play outdoors or indoors. (Put a big plastic tablecloth underneath when inside.) Or use it as a portable toy box indoors or out.

- Mend a torn mesh playpen with dental floss or fishing line.

- Turn an old piano bench into a play table for children to sit at on low stools or chairs. (Big ice-cream buckets do fine!) It even offers storage space!

- Use an old television stand or lazy Susan as a dollhouse stand.

- Spread out an old window shade as floor covering for children who are finger painting, coloring, or creating a toy car track. A flannel-backed vinyl tablecloth works well, too.

- Use a large old diaper pail as a laundry hamper.

- Put small game pieces in zip-lock bags to prevent them from getting lost and to reduce the risk of choking if younger children get into the games.

- Use plastic travel soap containers to store playing cards.

- Convert your child's baby "squeak" toys into hand puppets. Cut them off a little below the neck and attach a gathered piece of fabric.

Kids' Rooms: Walls

- Paint a growth chart on the wall or door frame for a visible, long-lasting record.

- Cut figures appropriate to your child's age and interests from self-adhesive vinyl. Press them onto a painted wall for economical wallpaper.

- Cover a wall section with shelf paper for drawing, or paint a wall or door with blackboard paint for your child to scribble on. Use a big old powder puff for an eraser. If crayon marks carry over onto a painted wall, remove them with toothpaste on a damp cloth. WD-40 or a hair dryer is also effective in softening the crayon wax before removing.

- Attach plain oilcloth to the wall with thumbtacks. It can be used as a blackboard, it wipes clean, and it's easily replaced when worn. Kids love to draw and paint on an artist's canvas, too, but it can't be washed clean.

- Make a bulletin board by cutting a section from a furniture or appliance box. Trim it neatly and add colorful masking tape or thin molding for a border.

- Put cork squares on the inside of the bedroom door. They serve the double purpose of muffling noise and providing bulletin board space.

Kids' Rooms: Furnishings

- Note that a low-pile, washable bathroom rug is practical for a small child's room. Indoor-outdoor carpeting is a good play surface, too.

- Consider installing track lighting to avoid the problem of lamps being overturned.

- Suspend a discarded lampshade from a ceiling light fixture, and attach small, no-longer-played-with toys with fine wire or fishing line for a decorative mobile.

- Avoid bunk beds until your child is dry all night. It's hard to change linens on upper and lower bunks. You might want to use sleeping bags instead of sheets and blankets when you do set up the bunks. Get fitted top sheets as well as bottom ones if you can find them. (Try a mail-order catalog, or make them if they're not available.)

- Speed up the chore of making bunk beds by making fitted spreads from regular bedspreads, to save tuck-in time. Use the extra fabric for pillow shams.

- Turn an old twin mattress or crib mattress into an extra bed for sleepover friends. Slide it under a regular bed for storage.

- Use bean-bag chairs or big foam pillows in older kids' rooms only. They can serve as building materials for forts as well as for sitting and tumbling. You might want to ban shoes in the bean-bag chair. A rip can be disastrous.

- Remove the closet door and put your child's bureau inside the closet to make the room look bigger and to create more play space.

Storing Stuff

The number of things a child accumulates seems to be directly proportional to the child's age. A new baby's clothes and toys take up a lot of space, but a toddler's take up even more.

Kids' Clothes

- Store a small child's socks in the bottom half of foam egg cartons that have been carefully washed and placed in drawers as dividers.

- Store underclothes, socks, T-shirts, and other small items in stackable plastic bins that are open in the front. They're easier for children to use than heavy bureau drawers.

- Cut out pictures of clothing items and tape them on the appropriate drawers to help children locate and put away their clothes.

- Fold your child's clothes in coordinating sets (matching shirt, pants, sweater, even socks).

Other Uses for Baby Wipe Containers

- Storing crayons and markers

- Storing trading cards

- Storing first-aid supplies

- As a piggy bank (Cut a slit in the top.)

- Storing recipe cards, photos, receipts, and so on

- Storing baby socks

- Storing sewing notions, buttons, and so on

Kids' Closets

- Make closet lights easy to turn on by tying bright-colored spools or old rattles to the pull chains or cords.

- Make a clothing rod at your child's height by hanging a broom handle from the regular rod at both ends with sturdy cord. The cord can be shortened to raise the rod as your child grows. Or use commercial rod extenders available in notions departments.

- Put a clothing hook on the back of your child's door for hanging pajamas and a robe.

- Keep a plastic garbage bag on a hanger in the closet. As clothes become outgrown or no longer worn, place them in the bag. When the time comes for a garage sale or donation, the sorting will already be done.

- Use lightweight, ventilated wire shelves and drawers. They're movable and adjustable and kids can see through them, which makes choosing clothes easier (and neater)!

Front Closet

- Assign each person a coat hook, and put up wicker baskets to hold caps, gloves, and scarves. Or attach a shoe rack or shoe bag to the inside wall to hold winter accessories.

- Glue clothespins with a hot glue gun to the inside of a closet door.

- Hang your umbrella stroller from a hook to keep it out of the way, or set it in your umbrella holder or a tall basket near the front door.

Organizing Kids' Toys

The trick is to accumulate the minimum—especially of toys with a million pieces. What you don't have, you don't have to store. How simple it sounds!

- Use horizontal rather than vertical storage wherever possible. Kids can get to toys more easily, and small items won't get lost or broken at the bottom of big chests or boxes.

- Build shelves of bricks and boards, but not so high that there's danger of toppling. The area underneath makes a nice "garage" for pull toys and cars, and the shelves above are good for books and toys.

- Put up a wooden pole with pegs from floor to ceiling, or use an expandable metal plant pole. Sew loops on stuffed animals and hang them on the pegs for neatness and decoration.

- Buy a package of small plastic rings from the fabric store, and sew them onto the ears of stuffed animals. They can then be hung on a houseplant pole within your child's reach. Or attach strips of Velcro horizontally on walls at your child's height, and sew or glue other strips on toys. Your child can "stick" toys away.

- Use a large plastic garbage can (with a lid) as an outdoor toy box. (Also works indoors!)

- Sew old (or new) sheer curtains together to make a see-through toy bag. Add a drawstring through the rod hem.

- Attach a hammock to the ceiling in a corner of your child's room to hold lots of toys that can be easily reached. Or improvise a hammock by folding a sheet or baby blanket into a triangle, tacking one point into the corner and the other two into the walls.

Organizers for Toys

- Small suitcases

- A large mailbox

- An old lunch box (for building blocks, small cars and trucks, or doll clothes; also works as a portable first-aid kit in your car)

- An old bassinet

- Laundry bags hung from wall hooks

- Plastic storage boxes or sweater boxes (Children can see what's inside.)

- Mesh laundry bags with tie or zippered closings

- A plastic wading pool

- Baskets attached to a wall

- Fishing tackle boxes

- A rolling wire mesh cart or stackable plastic basket with wheels

- Stackable plastic vegetable bins

- A plastic dish drainer (for books and records; the silverware section for pencils and crayons)

- A plastic dishpan for children's books

- Three, five, or seven 46-ounce cans or plastic ice-cream buckets glued together with open ends facing the same way, and spray painted (Set the assembly on its side, like a wine rack, to hold small toys or art materials.)

- A large plastic garbage can with a swing lid

- Large plastic ice-cream containers

- Large heavy boxes cut down and covered with Contact paper or wallpaper

- Disposable diaper boxes (Draw a picture or cut out a magazine photo of the item to be stored in the box. Tape it to the box so your child can easily see where certain toys should be stored.)

Toy Management

- Place a laundry basket next to the highchair to catch items thrown off the tray. You can pick them up all at once, and the cycle can start again.

- Hang a shoe bag in your child's playpen to store small toys. Putting them in and taking them out of the pockets will keep your baby amused.

- Buy an inexpensive storage box for your child's keepsakes. Store it under the bed.

- Attach a rope handle to a plastic laundry basket. Even a small child can easily pull it from room to room for playing and for quick pickups. (When your child is through with it, you can use it for your own purposes.)

- Encourage the parent of a visiting playmate to bring one or two of the child's favorite toys from home. This allows for trading of toys.

- Lay a bed sheet down on the floor to make picking up small pieces of building toys easier. When play is finished, pick up the sheet corners and pour the pieces into the container.

- Put away some of your child's toys for a few months. When you bring them out again, they'll be like new. Put other toys away as you bring ones out.

- Consider dividing toys among several plastic baskets and rotating them daily.

- Make putting away toys a game like "Auction." (You auction off the toys and your child puts them away.) Or say, "I see something in this room that is blue." Your child guesses the toy and then gets to put it away. Or play "Race." (You do a chore while your child puts away toys.)

- Give your child a chance to make a decision to part with a toy on occasion. For a child who tends to hoard belongings, you'll probably have to make the decision yourself.

- Label seven boxes or bags with names of the days of the week. Divide the toys among the boxes, and store them in a closet or other convenient place. Have your child play with the toys for the appropriate day. You'll have less to pick up, and your child will have "new" toys every day.

• Keep a pretty basket or bowl in the kitchen for toy odds and ends found throughout the day. You can return them to their appropriate places at the end of the day, and your child will know where to look for missing parts.

• Use fingernail polish to mark your child's toys before they're taken outside. There will be no question about which toy belongs to whom.

Toy Play Tips

• Make a soft toy snake out of one of Dad's old ties. Stuff it and sew up the ends. Make a triangle mouth on one end, and add buttons for eyes.

• Add a key ring with a decorative tab to your child's pull toys. It's easier to hold on to.

• Prevent strings on pull toys from getting caught in the wheels. Draw the string through a plastic straw or plastic tubing, then knot it to hold the straw in place next to the toy.

• Use an old baby bottle nipple to replace a round stopper lost from a piggy bank. The nipple has a lip that locks in the hole of the piggy bank, just like the original stopper.

• Stick tape on carpet to make "roads" for toy cars. When you're finished playing, pull up the tape and discard.

• Design a play "town" on a tight-weave, neutral carpet sample. Use permanent marker to draw roads wide enough for your child's cars. Add trees, homes, and buildings (gas station, library, grocery store, and so on).

• Buy shower curtain rings as an inexpensive alternative to plastic play links.

Chapter 5

The Challenge of Parenting

Perhaps the greatest challenge of parenting is helping our children become social human beings. We want them to become secure, competent, well-adjusted, polite, and independent people, but those qualities can't be developed by simply following a formula. Our children's unique personalities and our own, plus all the other factors in our particular situations, combine to further complicate the already complicated process of growing up.

Manners

Setting a good example in social situations is important. "Do as I say, not as I do," doesn't wash, even with little children. In order to cut down the use of *no* in front of others (and alone at home, too), some parents try to say *yes*, with qualifications. "Yes, you may have a cookie after dinner." "Yes, you may play outdoors after you nap."

Being Quiet

- Choose front-row seats at religious services or other gatherings where children are apt to be noisy or fidgety. Knowing they can be seen helps some children behave well, and most enjoy being able to see what's going on.

- Or sit in back, where you can make a quick getaway if necessary. Some say to exit only when absolutely necessary and to return as soon as potty duty has been accomplished or screaming has stopped.

• Seat a child between two adults at a meeting or service.

• Teach your children to whisper—a technique that must be learned before you take them to places where loud talking isn't permissible. There's "outside voice" (loud) and "inside voice" (soft).

• Find little jobs for children to do when they must be quiet at services or meetings. They can keep track of how many times the rabbi or minister says "God," or they can count the number of children in each row of seats.

• Bring an assortment of quiet toys your child can play with at a meeting or service. One possibility is a stack of fabric scraps pinned together. Or take a spool of thread along, and break off short lengths for your child to play with, if she's old enough to know not to eat them.

• Bring quiet food, if necessary, such as raisins.

Table Talk

• Teach your children to modulate their voices by recording them on tape and playing it back so they can hear their stridency.

• Serving dinner by candlelight seems to lower voices. There's nothing wrong with lighting candles nightly!

• Establish a series of signals for correcting table manners. For example, saying, "Twenty-two," is less annoying for children and makes correcting them away from home less obvious. (Some parents say this practice becomes a game for older children, who sometimes enjoy putting their parents through a little exercise in calling numbers.)

• Ask a whining child to repeat his request in a regular voice. Or squint your face and let your child know your ears hurt (and don't work) when exposed to that tone of voice. Or let your child know that whining is okay but only in his bedroom.

The Proper Response

- Don't respond to your child's "Huh?" once you've explained that it's more polite to say "Pardon me?"

- Don't let go of an item you're offering your child until you hear "Please" or "Thank you." Ignore an interrupting child until "Excuse me" is said.

- Have weekly or monthly tea parties. Use nice (not expensive) dishes and napkins, and play classical music. It's a special event that gives you the opportunity to teach and practice valuable social skills.

- Apologize for your own lapses, and ask your children to do the same.

Telephone Interruptions

You can minimize calls by screening them with Caller ID or an answering machine or by letting your answering service take a message. You can also have little talks about manners. Or you can pace about, maintaining order while you're talking. But the interruptions probably won't stop until your child is old enough to make and receive calls—and realize the importance of quiet while someone's on the phone. In the meantime, there are some things you can try.

- Take advantage of the time to hold and cuddle your child.

- Allow water play in the sink if you're talking in the kitchen and can keep an eye on your child.

- Keep a special box of toys or a pad of paper and a few crayons near the phone, to be played with only while you're talking. Or let your child rummage through your handbag (minus lipstick and any sharp items).

- Get your child a toy phone to talk on while you're on your phone. Or give him an unplugged real phone.

- Let your child make a phone call by himself! Dial the number your child wants to call, then hang up and let your child press the redial button. Or use the memory buttons on your phone.

- Teach your child to raise his hand or place it on his head (or do some other signal) if it's really necessary to interrupt you. You can terminate the call or ask the other party to hold for a moment while you take care of your child.

- Teach your child the signal for when you *must not be* interrupted. Stand up for uninterruptible calls; sit down for calls that can be interrupted. Consider using a timer to show your child how much time is left (and to shorten your conversations).

- *Occasionally* let your child say hello to your caller. (You'll be sorry if you make it a habit!) Make sure it's someone who won't mind, like Grandma.

- Avoid lengthy phone calls, or schedule them during naptime.

- Make long-distance calls when your child is nearby, to keep them short!

- Use a cordless phone so you can play with your child while finishing your conversation.

Telephone Safety Tips

- Pick up your active baby to go with you when you need to leave the room to answer the phone or door. It takes only a few seconds for a child to get into trouble.

- Hang the phone cord on a cup hook screwed into the wall above the phone, so your child can't pull on it.

- Hold down contact points on the phone with wide rubber bands, to keep your child from disconnecting you or accidentally dialing South Africa.

- Place a red dot by the 0 for Operator. Be certain your young child knows how to push the 0 button and ask for help. When your child is old enough to use the phone responsibly, teach how to dial 911 in an emergency.

Tantrums

Most parents believe it's best to ignore tantrums whenever possible. When there's no audience, there's no need to perform. Many caution, though, that it's important not to ignore the child. They ask themselves if they're enforcing too-rigid standards, holding too-high expectations, or not giving enough TLC. Try to avoid the tantrum point by preventing your child from becoming overtired or frustrated. Help with a toy that won't work, insist on a short rest, or offer a little snack. Any of these may avert a tantrum you see coming.

Dealing with Temper Tantrums

- Let your child scream to his heart's content sometimes (outdoors, perhaps, if you live in the country). Everybody needs to let off steam occasionally.

- Tell your child firmly that the rule still stands (if discipline precipitated the tantrum), then ignore the tantrum.

- Try to distract your child by doing or saying something unusual or silly. You might even stage your own mock tantrum and ask your child if you're doing it right. Or turn the lights on and off rapidly—another attention-getter. Some parents say (if you can do this without anger or hostility) to slowly pour a glass of water over a child's head for *real* drama! (Recommended *only* in the kitchen or bathroom.)

- Pick up your child and gently shake the "mads" in a fun way.

- Disappear! If you're in another room, you'll feel better, and the tantrum will probably be short-lived. If your child follows you, move again.

- Ask your child to go to his room and stay there until the lost "happy face" is found.

- Stop breath-holding by gently blowing into your child's face, dashing a small amount of cold water on his face, or applying a cold washcloth. Don't panic if your child starts to become cyanotic (turns blue or purple due to lack of oxygen in the blood). Fainting automatically stops breath-holding.

- Escort your child calmly to the car or a restroom if a tantrum occurs when you're away from home. When the tantrum subsides, return to the business at hand. If you can't leave, simply let the tantrum continue, and grit your teeth.

Handling Inappropriate Behavior

- Set a timer, and tell your child that the behavior must stop when the bell rings. Or tell your child you're going to count to ten, then start counting out loud. Be prepared to enforce the consequences (like leaving the store) when you're finished counting. Empty threats don't work.

- Call out a funny magic phrase such as "Un-gah-wah!" which is your family's secret signal to *stop* whatever activity is going on. Use it in nondisciplinary situations occasionally, such as during a game, and be prepared to have it used on you.

- Praise your child for good self-control and good sense when the misbehavior stops.

- Choose a "time out" location where your child must go when misbehavior doesn't stop. Have your child remain there for a designated period of time. (Many parents choose one minute for each year of age.) This not only ends the behavior, it gives your child a chance to calm down and stop the momentum that may have gotten out of control. Be prepared to redirect your child's attention to a positive activity when the time out ends.

Calming an Angry Child

- Hold your small child tightly while rocking and singing. Express your love in terms of increasing size. For example, "My love for you is as big as a flower...as big as a teacup...as big as a bush...." Try to get your child involved in thinking up bigger and bigger things.

- Whisper in your child's ear. If you can think of something really good to whisper, your child's mood may change altogether.

- Tell your child there's a smile inside, and if it's not let out, it will turn into a giggle. (It often will.) Mimic your child exaggeratedly and say, "No laughing!" (Don't forget to talk about the problem when the giggling is over.)

- Scold a piece of furniture or a toy that "causes" the trouble. Your child will probably end up laughing.

- Lend your child a hug and a kiss when things are going well; call in the loan when anger strikes. This gives your child a chance to express warmth and calm down so you can talk about the problem.

- Help your child calm down after a crying spree by taking deep breaths together. Pretend your child's toes are candles that have to be blown out using deep breaths.

Helping a Child Vent Anger

Children, like adults, shouldn't be required to hold anger in all the time. You may want to talk with your child about anger, including the words used to express it, and show your understanding.

- Encourage your child to vent anger physically by running around outdoors, by punching a big batch of play dough, or by hitting a tree with a stick.

- Teach your child to count to five in a loud, angry voice, to play an angry song on a musical instrument, or to dance an angry dance. Or shout something loudly with your child, and let your voices drop gradually until there's silence.

- Have your child draw a picture of these angry feelings.

- Help your child deal with anger by creating a Rage Rock. Pick out a rock together, paint it, then have your child squeeze it when angry. Keep it in a convenient location.

Sibling Rivalry

The only way to prevent sibling rivalry is to have only one child. A certain amount of jealousy and squabbling is normal between siblings. It's impossible to make a child stop feeling emotions like jealousy and the need to win. Knowing that there are times when you dislike someone you love is realistic and healthy.

It's usually best to let children work things out themselves, since most fighting is done to prod parents into doing something. Of course, there are times when you must interfere for safety's sake or when you just can't stand any more fighting!

Fair Is Fair

- Make sure your children have rights to their *own* things. It's hard for them to share if they're not secure and guilt-free about ownership. Allow them not to share certain things, if they wish.

- Don't label a child "selfish" or show disapproval over unwillingness to share. Make a point of sharing yourself, and make sure your children see you doing it.

- Tell your child who doesn't want to share, "When you're finished playing with the toy, your sister (or brother) may have it." This lets your child know someone's waiting, but eliminates the distress of giving up the toy immediately.

- Let one child cut the cake or divide the treat, and let the other child get first pick, if they're fighting about fairness.

- Set a timer to ring when it's time to exchange toys.

- Assign each child a special day or days (like Monday, Wednesday, and Friday) when the child can make certain decisions, select menus, be first at something, and so on.

- Play the "Stone Game." Put a small stone in one hand; the child who picks the correct hand gets first choice.

- Avoid fights over similar objects such as pails, shovels, and balls by assigning a color to each child and buying those items in the assigned colors.

- Use a bookcase or piece of furniture to divide a bedroom shared by squabblers. Divide the closet by painting each side a different color.

- If worse comes to worst, hang a sign outside to tell the world your kids are fighting (when they're old enough to be embarrassed). Take it in when they stop.

Changing the Pace

- Suggest a new activity when your kids are squabbling a lot. Boredom often leads to quarrels.

- Try distraction when you see that an older child is getting frustrated with a younger one. Say, "Quick, I need you! Please come help me."

- Spray glass cleaner on the inside and outside of a sliding glass door or a ground-level window. Place your fighting children on opposite sides, and give each one a dry cloth. By the time the glass is dry, the kids will be laughing.

- End a verbal argument by having your kids sing their complaints to each other.

- Ask your kids for ideas to solve the problem. Let them think of special ways they can accommodate each other. Even if their ideas don't ultimately work, your kids will be trying to resolve their differences.

- Get out the camera and take a pretend (or actual) photo of your kids "fighting," to diffuse the situation. Then take a picture of them hugging. Let them mug for another photo, if they want to.

- Get up and leave the house, if you can, or at least consider the bathroom as a refuge. Like temper tantrums, fighting often stops when there's no audience.

- Send each quarreling child to a different corner of the room, and have them sit facing each other. Tell them they must speak calmly and stay put until they give each other permission to leave. Negotiations usually lead to peace.

- Have quarreling children mention five nice qualities about each other. Mutual compliments often end the war.

- Remove the object of disagreement, or separate your children. Not being allowed to play together (or with a disputed toy) may motivate them to resolve their differences.

Kicking Habits

Habits that parents don't like aren't necessarily bad ones; more often they're just annoying. Some are established as responses to frustration or anxiety, others as tension relievers to provide security in a confusing world. Some parents find that ignoring a habit helps, if no one is being hurt; others try to get to the bottom of things. Remember, *you* can't break your child's habit, but you can help your *child* break it.

The Pacifier

- Put pickle juice or something else sour or bitter on the pacifier, so it won't taste good.

- "Lose" the pacifier if your child is sixteen months or older. At that age, a child will probably understand the concept of losing things, and won't question the fact that the "crutch" is gone.

- Suggest that some new baby might appreciate the pacifier now that your child is so grown-up.

- Start a little hole in the pacifier and enlarge it a bit every few days until the shape and taste are no longer appealing. Or cut the end off so it can't be used.

- Tell your child that when this last pacifier is lost or worn out, there will be no more. The advance notice may make the end easier.

- Wean your child off a pacifier slowly by first restricting its use from one room, then in more rooms, then in every room except the bedroom, then only at naptime and bedtime, and so on.

- Try to coordinate giving up the pacifier with giving up the regular nap, if possible. (Remember that if you get your child to give up the pacifier, the nap may go too, whether you like it or not!) A very tired child will go to sleep quickly at night and probably won't miss the pacifier so much.

Thumb Sucking

Many parents say, "Don't try to stop it; thumb sucking fulfills a need for comfort and security and is not necessarily a manifestation of unusual tension or frustration." I'm partial to the mother who said, "Ignore it. Sucking is a basic need. Orthodontia is less expensive than psychiatry." Some dentists feel that if it continues for a long time (after age four), thumb or finger sucking can change the shape of a child's mouth and put permanent teeth out of alignment—a good reason for regular dental checkups. Yet one neighbor told me, "My child sucked his thumb but my neighbor's four did not. Who needed braces? All of them!" If you want to see it stopped, there are things to try.

- Try giving your baby a pacifier as a substitute. Some dentists say the Nuk pacifier will not ruin tooth alignment. It's easier to wean a child from a pacifier than from a thumb.

- Try some physical means of stopping the thumb sucking, such as a bad-tasting solution from the drugstore that you put on the thumb. (Some parents caution that if children rub their eyes, the stuff will sting.)

- Sew mitts to pajama sleeves, or buy or make finger puppets for your child to wear while sleeping.

- Put a kiss in each of your child's hands at bedtime. Tell your child to hold them closed all night to keep the kisses in.

- Restrict older children's thumb sucking to their rooms. The desire can then be indulged, and you don't have to see it. Chances are that being with you will become more important than the habit.

- Ask your dentist to warn your child about possible future dental problems. The voice of a neutral party often carries more weight than that of a parent. (This can also work for a pacifier.)

Biting

Children bite for different reasons, usually depending on their ages. Biting isn't motivated by aggressive feelings. Those who bite don't intend to hurt any more that a toddler who shoves and hits as part of normal play. For a baby, biting may simply be a new tactile experience. For a one- to two-year-old, biting can be a great attention-getting device and is usually done out of frustration.

Biting can also be a way of getting another child to back off. High stress levels and feeling overpowered by older children can lead a child to bite. The child who bites in anger or frustration usually outgrows the habit when old enough to verbalize his problems. It's also possible that a child is imitating another biter—human or otherwise. Whatever the cause, vigilance is recommended until the habit is outgrown or "cured." The focus should be on prevention rather than reaction.

- Dramatize your pain and sorrow at being bitten; your child's sympathy may rise to the top. (If your child seems to think this is a marvelous game, try another tactic!)

- Try to involve your child in comforting the bitten child by applying ice, for example.

- Remove your child from your lap or the room, and explain that biting is not acceptable.

- Say, "No biting!" while holding your child's jaw with your thumb and index finger. (Apply only light pressure.)

- Give your child something that *can* be bitten, such as a rubber teething toy or soft doll. Or an apple or a bagel!

- Put your child's arm in his mouth and encourage a "self-bite" to show how much it really hurts. Or place your thumb on your child's bottom lip and firmly press down against his teeth while saying, "This is what it feels like when you bite."

Dawdling

Dawdling is just a form of negativism that most children pick up between age two and three. Be patient; it passes.

- Set a timer in your child's room, and make it a game to be washed and dressed before the timer rings. Or set one to ring in the kitchen for when it's time to leave the house.

- Give your child an alarm clock to help instill a sense of responsibility about getting up. Be lavish with praise when responsibility is shown.

- Don't serve breakfast to a child in pajamas; one who's dressed is ready to eat!

- Keep breakfast simple and interesting. Leftover pizza is one option.

- Offer limited choices (either "this" or "that") rather than asking your children what they want to do, wear, or eat.

- Don't turn on the TV until your child is dressed, in order to keep distractions to a minimum.

- Encourage your child to hurry up by reminding her of the fun things that may happen that day.

- Let a dawdler miss an activity or depart in pajamas, if possible. Chances are your child will be ready the next time.

Fears and Tears

The apparent fear that babies show by turning away from anyone other than a parent is nothing to apologize for or worry about—it's a sign of mental and emotional development. Toddlers and older children learn fear when they realize they can't control some things. They may be afraid of being hurt or of being abandoned at bedtime or when left with a sitter.

Teasing and shaming a fearful child may cause him to hide his fear behind belligerence—or to give up and become withdrawn. It's important to *listen* carefully to a child to find out exactly what the child is afraid of.

Facing Up to Fears

- Reintroduce an eight- or nine-month-old to the vacuum cleaner, if fear of it develops. Carry your child with you as you vacuum, let her push the on-off switch, and let her help push the vacuum.

- Do something physical about irrational fears such as fear of "monsters." (Some parents think magical things should be dealt with magically.) Spray them away with a spray bottle filled with water, or use an atomizer filled with cologne. (Your child will smell "monster repellent" after you're gone.) Blow them out the window, flush them down the toilet, throw them in the garbage, have the family pet come in to eat them, or recite a homemade incantation against them before leaving the room. (Other parents disagree. They say that such actions reinforce the fear, because a parent seems to believe in monsters, too. They feel that saying, "There are no monsters, except in make-believe," is better.)

- Treat all fears seriously, and do what you can to alleviate them. For example, if your child is afraid of shadows on the wall caused by outside traffic, take the trouble to move the bed to a "safer" wall, or get an opaque shade.

- Play a game of "What if" to rehearse the handling of a scary event. For example, explain to your child what she should do if she gets lost, if the lights go out, if she has to go to the doctor, if you or your partner gets sick, and so on.

- Tell your child about fears you had as a child and how you overcame them. Or ask your parents to tell your child stories about your childhood fears.

- Have your child draw a picture of what's bothering her. Or draw a picture yourself of what you think is wrong, and have your child tell you if it's correct. Change the picture somehow to convert the negative to a positive. For example, put a smile on the monster.

The Security Blanket

Don't let your child think a blanket or other "lovey" is bad. Security objects help ease the transition to independence, and they symbolize your child's ability to develop an interest in things outside himself.

- Cut a favorite blanket in half as soon as your child becomes attached to it. Whisk the dirty half away for laundering when your child's not looking, and replace it with the clean half. With luck, your child will never realize there are two blankets.

- Try to promote a cloth diaper as a security blanket; a clean one is always available.

- Cut up an old nightgown into small pieces, if your child has always loved its softness. The pieces won't drag on the floor, and there'll be a good supply of clean ones.

- Consider saving the shreds of a security blanket once your child no longer needs it. They've been included in more than one wedding bouquet!

Fear of the Dark

- Take a nighttime walk up and down your block in good weather to teach your child that the dark is magical, not spooky. Or lie on a blanket in your yard looking at the stars, watching for fireflies, and listening to night sounds.

- There's no law that says your child can't sleep with a light on. Provide an easy nightlight by replacing the bulb in a regular lamp with a small, colored bulb. Or consider a lighted fish tank that your child can watch until asleep.

- For a child who fears monsters under the bed, remove the frame and put the mattress and box spring directly on the floor.

- Hang a picture of a police officer to "patrol" your child's bedroom at night. You can find these pictures at your local school supplies store. Or hang a poster of your child's favorite television or movie character to "guard" your child's room.

- Explain that sheets (or quilts) are magic blankets that protect children.

- Place glow-in-the-dark stars, moons, and planets on the bedroom ceiling. Tell your child to pick one star, make a wish, and concentrate on that star.

- Play soft, soothing music for your child to fall asleep to.

- Keep a flashlight near your child's bed.

- Promise to check back in a few minutes (ten or so), and do so. Ask if everything is okay, and say that you'll be back again. Continue until your child is reassured that you're around and checking.

Nightmares

- Make sure a child who has had a bad dream is completely awake. Talk to your child soothingly and reassuringly, and insist on an answer that shows she's fully awake.

- Take your child to the bathroom. It's probably a good idea anyway, and it will ensure complete wakefulness.

- Turn your child's pillow over and say, "Good dreams happen on *this* side."

- Encourage your child to change "dream channels" in her head.

- Talk a little about the dream, explaining that it was only a dream and not reality. The next day, talk more about it, and discuss the fact that dreams are marvelous experiences over which a person can have some control. If something's chasing you, for example, you can turn around and chase it.

Fear of Thunder

- Play marching music to cheer up a child who's afraid of thunderstorms. The loudness of the music will drown out the thunder, and marching will give your child something active to do.

- *Boom* back at the thunder.

- See if you and your child can sing a whole verse of a song or recite the whole alphabet before the next thunderclap.

- Decorate an "emergency thunderstorm box" with magazine photos of clouds, rain, lightning, and so on. Fill the cardboard box with small inexpensive games, puzzles, and markers, and store it in your child's closet. Take it out only when it's thundering, to shift your child's focus away from the storm.

- Say, "Look, God's taking our picture!"

Leave-Taking without Tears

You shouldn't feel guilty about going out once in a while. Both parents and children are happier with occasional separations. Children are smart enough to pick up on parents' guilt and play "poor me." Some parents sneak out while their child is occupied; others say, "*Never* do that!" Don't ask your child for permission to leave either. Many parents leave for only a short period of time when a new sitter is on duty.

Starting at about six months, young babies begin to fear separation from their parents because they don't understand that separation won't be permanent. At this time, tears and anxiety are not only normal, they're positive signs that a warm and loving relationship has developed. The techniques below work for sitters, daycare providers, and even grandparents.

For the Very Young

- Play "Peek a Boo" frequently to help a little one understand that you can disappear and still return.

- Use distraction to divert your baby's attention away from your departure.

- Show physical affection to reassure your baby; have your sitter do the same.

- Bring a security blanket, book, or favorite toy to a sitter's house. Or make a surprise bag containing items to be opened after you leave.

- Establish a good-bye ritual. For example, hug and kiss your child before leaving, wave good-bye from the doorway, and honk your horn as you drive away.

- Have the sitter come fifteen to thirty minutes early so an activity can get started before you leave.

- Spend a few minutes with your child before you leave, instead of rushing off. This applies to daycare situations as well as at home.

- Videotape yourself at home doing chores, reading a book, or singing songs, so your child can watch you when you're not there.

Additional Help for Separation Anxiety

- Kiss your child's palm and close the fingers into a fist. Explain that if there's a need for a kiss, there's one in there ready and waiting. Plant a lipstick kiss on your child's hand for the same effect.

- Keep family photos handy so your child can look at them for reassurance. Let your child take a family photo to daycare.

- Remind your child that you will always come back, and try to be back when you said you would. Call if you're delayed, and explain the problem to your child directly if she's old enough to talk on the phone.

- Tell a child who doesn't understand about time that you'll be back "after snack time" instead of "in three hours." For a child who's a little older, set a play clock with your return time so your child can compare it with one that's running. For a child going to daycare or preschool, send along a paper-plate clock showing the pickup time. Your child can compare it with the clock on the wall.

- Give your child something of yours to take care of or wear until you return, such as a bracelet, photograph, or small mirror.

- Give your child plenty of advance warning, if possible. Talk about who will take care of your child and what exciting things they will do. Avoid promising something that hasn't been arranged with the sitter.

- When going on vacation without your kids, give them a sense of when you'll be back by filling paper lunch bags with treats (coloring books, crayons, and so on) for each day you'll be gone. When the last bag has been opened, they'll know you'll be home that day.

Developing Self-Esteem

Parents who want their children to develop high self-esteem make a point of treating them with respect and courtesy. They don't reserve "Please," "Thank you," and "I'm sorry" for adults. They don't belittle their children, and they correct or punish them in private when they can, to help their kids save face. And they advise, "Don't take it all too seriously. No single incident will shape your child's character!"

Making Children Feel Special by Word

- Use your child's name often in conversation, and use nicknames only if your child really likes them. Use your child's name in other ways, too (wooden letters on the wall of your child's room, magnetic letters on the refrigerator, a sign on the door, a puzzle, a homemade place mat, and so on).

- Designate a special song for each member of the family. Making up your own words can make it even more special.

- Share a special secret with each child. It could be a "middle child" secret (if both parent and child qualify) or a code word that no one else knows.

- Tell your child to give himself a pat on the back for something done well. (Children need to learn to affirm themselves, since parents won't always be there to do it.)

...And by Deed

- Tape-record your child's voice while she's singing, reciting, or talking with you. Play it back for your child, expressing your delight at her verbal skills.

- Keep a running list on the refrigerator door of positive things your child has done that day. Read the list at bedtime to help your child feel good about herself before going to sleep.

- Keep a joint diary with your child. Have her contribute to the content and provide illustrations wherever she likes. Cover the pages with clear Contact paper to preserve them. Occasionally read a page or two to your child at bedtime.

- Share baby record books and photo albums with your older children, so they can enjoy their growth and development.

- Keep a "baby" drawer or box for archiving anecdotes and keepsakes from your child's life. Add to it as often as you like, including the letter you wrote to your unborn child while you were pregnant. The drawer or box may also serve as a place to store your child's artwork as she grows older. Going through the box once or twice a year will be fun for all!

- Let your kids entertain you with plays they make up. Give them wooden spoons or mixing beaters to use as "microphones," and prepare to clap a lot as they ham it up!

- Create an impression! Cut around your child's hand in cookie dough to make handprint cookies, or make a large picture by tracing an outline of your child's body on paper or cardboard and then cutting it out.

Specials for Fathers

In spite of the fact that *dada* is one of the first words a baby learns (often inspired by Mom, who wants to make Dad feel good), fathers often spend comparatively less time with their children when they're small. Today more and more fathers are finding that they want to have a more meaningful influence on their children's lives, and many have developed special things to do.

- Take advantage of your natural inclination to get down on the floor and play with your child. Even a new baby will like lying on your chest, and floor play can be a special father-child time.

- Share your morning shave time with your child. Make a shaving cream beard on your child's face, and have your child (girl or boy) shave it off with a plastic spoon or an old credit card that's been cut into the shape of a razor.

- Write down your feelings periodically about being a parent and about how you see your children. You'll like looking back on your writings, and so will your children when they're old enough.

- Visit your parents with one child at a time, leaving your partner and other children at home. It's excellent one-on-one time, plus your parents may seldom get to see you without your partner.

- Give your time, rather than "things." Write down a list of activities you and your child enjoy together, and let your child choose one when a reward is in order.

- Bring a memento home from a business trip, but be aware that it need not be an expensive present. The small soaps, shower caps, and shoe-cleaning cloths from hotels are always appreciated, as are airline magazines, plastic utensils from meals, and packets of sugar or condiments.

- Write notes or letters to your children if you must depart before they wake up.

Building Self-Esteem in the Family

- Start your day earlier so you and your family will be less stressed. You can also make the mornings easier by getting things ready the night before.

- Let each child do something alone with just one parent occasionally.

- Say at least one positive, affirming thing to your child every day.

- Provide an alternative pleasure for a younger child if an older one has something special planned. For example, if the older one is invited to sleep over at a friend's house, your little one might be allowed to sleep in the sibling's bed.

- Expect your children to do as much as they can as well as they can, and let them know you expect this. But also let them know that it's okay to make mistakes sometimes; mistakes (even Mom's and Dad's) show people ways to learn and improve.

- Find additional creative ideas in my books *101 Ways to Make Your Child Feel Special* and *101 Ways to Tell Your Child "I Love You"* (Contemporary/McGrawHill, 800–255–3379).

Social Skills

Learning to live and play with others is a lifelong task. Children begin to learn social skills by interacting with family members and people outside the family. While school plays an important role in developing social skills, learning starts well before children are off to school. Group daycare and preschool are often important influences, as are play dates and playgroups.

Playgroups are informal associations parents put together for kids. Sometimes they include both parents and children; other times kids rotate from house to house with each set of parents taking a turn watching the group. In either case, parents are not required to pay for their children's care. Playgroups often work best with kids ages four to eight, with participating families living fairly close together. Check the Internet to learn more about how playgroups might work for you.

Play dates usually involve one or two children. As with playgroups, play dates may or may not involve all the parents. Except for biting and hitting, when you must intervene, let the kids work out their disputes.

Making Play Dates Work

Play dates can occur with or without a second parent around. A child's "separation anxiety" quotient will be your determining factor.

- Help your child select a playmate with similar interests (dinosaurs, Barbies, and so on) so they'll be more likely to have fun.

- Planning one play date a week is usually sufficient.

- Take your child's nap schedule into account. You may have to limit play dates to children who are on a similar nap schedule.

- Take preventive measures to minimize conflict by asking your child to put away hard-to-share toys. Take out duplicate toys, and talk to your child about sharing before playmates comes over.

- Start with a snack if children are coming from preschool or another group setting.

- Start playtime with one planned activity, and let them go from there.

- Have the children meet at a neutral setting, such as a park or playground, if you don't have the time or inclination to clean up at home.

- Try to keep your child's siblings out of the play date activities, if possible.

- Limit play dates to an hour or two. (Start with a half hour and build up.)

- Plan on taking your child's playmates home, if you can. Creating a good and timely end to the play date can influence its success.

Transition from Worker to Parent

Leaving work at work is very hard when you first go back. It gets easier over time, but it usually remains one of the biggest challenges working parents face. Thinking yourself into the proper parenting frame of mind on your way home can help. Listen to a parenting or self-help tape to set the stage.

- Before leaving work, make a list of things you have to do the next day. That way you won't have to think about them when you're at home.

- Call home and leave messages to remind yourself of things you need to do once you get home.

- If you ride a bus, get off before your usual stop so you can get some walking time in. Or run errands before picking up your child or arriving home.

- Try to allow for some "hanging around" time (ten minutes or so) when picking up your child from daycare or preschool, rather than rushing home or to your next errand. This will give you time to focus much-needed attention on your child.

- Change out of your work clothes and into your most comfortable outfit as soon as your get home, so you can begin to relax.

- Make a snack or some appetizers to relieve hunger pangs for you and your child. This will give you more time to relax before beginning to prepare dinner.

- Put your baby or small child in the tub with you, if a bath is your key to relaxing. It will give you and your child a chance to unwind and play together.

- Have a neighborhood teen come over for an hour or so after you get home, to help with dinner or play with the kids.

- Make an "appointment" for one-on-one time with an older child at a specific time later in the evening, so your child is assured of access to you.

- Make arrangements with your partner to alternate after-work childcare demands. Take the kids one day and have your partner take them the next, so you can care take of yourself at least every other day after work.

Chapter 6

Family Heritage

Giving your child a sense of belonging to a special, important group—a family, large or small—is one of the nicest things you can do. One way of developing this sense is to help your child know all the members of the family and their relationships to one another (not always easy, the way some families are scattered today). Another is to observe family traditions. And then there's keeping track of it all. Even today, with the large number of single parents, family life is possible and necessary. Ex-spouses need encouragement so they don't become ex-parents. Children need all the parents and extended family they can get.

Being Part of the Clan

Even when family members live nearby, children sometimes get confused about the relationships. And, of course, there are friends who become members of our family. Your efforts to give your child a sense of belonging to a clan will help provide a feeling of importance and a clearer self-image.

Understanding Relationships

Who's who? Many families make a point of discussing family relationships often. "Grandma is my mommy; Uncle Roger is Daddy's brother." It's both instructive and fun to reminisce about family history and to talk about current family events.

- Put together a family of dolls or paper dolls to help your child understand relationships.

- Draw a family tree on shelf paper, or paint one on a wall in your child's room. Attach photos of relatives.

- Devise different names for two sets of grandparents, to help children distinguish them: Grandma and Grandpa for one set, for example, and Grammy and Poppy for the other. Or add first names or surnames. Some grandparents like to choose their own names.

- Use photos to help acquaint your children with relatives. Put together an album and look at it together often. Give children photo cubes of their own. Or post photos on the refrigerator or bulletin board.

"Relative" Activities

Nothing can quite replace visits for getting to know one's relatives. If your family enjoys big get-togethers on holidays or family reunions, your children are especially lucky. Imaginative use of the telephone, mail, computer (for e-mail), video camera (digital or other), VCR, and audiotape recorder can provide good substitutes for visits and gatherings.

- Let one child at a time spend the night with grandparents, if they live close by. The grandparents can serve a meal the child likes, and the child can explore the grandparents' home and learn their routines.

- Give grandparents a photo album containing a new grandchild's photos and other memorabilia (such as first drawings). Ask grandparents to write in the album about their memories of the child. The visiting child will have his own special book to look at over the years.

- Post photos of relatives near the phone so your children can see the relative they're talking to. Or make a telephone book for your child using photos instead of written names.

- Personalize any card game from "Go Fish" to "Concentration" by cutting up duplicate photos of family members and attaching them to the backs of the playing cards with clear packing tape. (Use at least two of any person.)

- Consider joining a "Rent a Grandparent" program through a church, synagogue, or retirement center, if your child rarely sees any older relatives.

Keeping Close to Faraway Relatives

- Find the homes of faraway relatives on a map. Do a little research on their cities or countries, and ask them to send photos of their homes, gardens, and neighborhoods.

- Get a large, sturdy puzzle of the United States, and let your child carry around the piece representing the state a relative lives in.

- Let your children send special artwork to grandparents and cousins. Or photocopy your child's hand, and send the handprint with a note to relatives. Your child is likely to get mail back, which will make those family members seem very special.

- Encourage faraway grandparents to send notes, cards, and inexpensive gifts by mail, in addition to calling. Small children aren't usually able to carry on very interesting telephone conversations.

- Let your child contribute a scribble, a picture, and eventually a full signature to your letters to relatives. You can take dictation from your child, too.

- Make video- and audiotapes, and send them to grandparents and other relatives. Mail the tapes back and forth so you get updates from both sides. If relatives don't have a VCR, they probably have friends who do.

- Send "kisses" to faraway grandparents. Let children put on lipstick and use their lips to decorate a piece of paper. Sign their name, laminate, and send off!

- Make an activities book for faraway grandparents. Load up the camera and take photos of the events that make up your child's typical week. Paste the photos into a book along with samples of handiwork. (A photo of your child painting could be accompanied by the painting itself.) Have your child dictate while you write on the opposite page. Call it "A Week in My Life," and add a dedication page (to the grandparents, of course).

• Don't let newer electronic gizmos stop you from using "old-fashioned" ideas like the ones above.

Making Grandparents Feel Special

Grandchildren provide the opportunity to redefine and enrich your relationship with your parents. You now have a new common bond—a love for your children. Remember that grandparents are entitled to different values based on different life experiences. It's normal for grandparents and parents to have different parenting styles.

Try to spend some one-on-one time with your parents—in fact, with each of your parents separately without anyone else along. As much as a grandparent loves a grandchild, the chance to have a special relationship with an adult child (especially one who made him or her a grandparent) is special.

• Take lots of photos of your parents with your children when they're babies. They will become your most valued keepsakes.

• Whenever you take your parents' advice, let them know. (They'll be pleased. Who wouldn't be?)

• Plant a tree or shrub in your parents' (or children's) honor in your yard with everyone present. Photograph your parents and children next to the tree on an annual basis. Think of it as giving "roots" as well as providing a visual history.

• Encourage your children to run with open arms to give Grandma and Grandpa a big hug each time they see them.

• Have your children ask your parents about your childhood years and what you were like as a youngster.

• Send your mother-in-law a thank-you note for raising such a wonderful person—your spouse!

Connecting Electronically

- Get Grandma and Grandpa and other long-distance relatives online for e-mail, e-photos, and e-video clips. E-mail is well suited for young children, who like the quick turnaround.

- Invest in a digital video camera so you can send short video clips of your children to your parents' computer. Some digital cameras can take twenty-to-thirty-second video clips, which is really all you need. These will then circulate to other relatives and friends. Encourage grandparents to do the same so your children can see how Grandma and Grandpa are doing.

- Invest in some inexpensive, webcam video-conferencing cameras and software so you can do "real time" talking with relatives and friends.

Traditions

Some traditions go back generations; others begin when a new family is established. A tradition can be as simple as the daily gathering at the dinner table to share the day's events, or as complex as a holiday celebration complete with special menus and observances. Beware of inflexibility in traditions. When a tradition is outgrown, store it in your memory and let it go!

Birthday Specials

Some parents help small children keep track of the days before a birthday by describing them as so many "sleeps" away or by making a paper chain and letting the child tear a link off each day. Remember that for a young child a year is an eternity, so consider having "half birthdays" twice a year. And for the child whose birthday falls on or near a major holiday, select (with the child's help) another day for the birthday party.

- Make a lunch date with a child who's in daycare or preschool, and continue the practice as your child grows up. Go to a special restaurant or have lunch at your workplace if you work outside your home.

- Plant a tree, shrub, or perennial plant as a lasting memory of your child's birthday. Let your child make the choice.

- Give your child a gift each year to add to a collection you started in early childhood (coins, shells, stamps, sports cards, small cars, and so on).

- Write a birthday letter to your child each year, noting highlights of the year, changes in your child, special accomplishments, and so on. These letters will become valuable keepsakes.

- Create a birthday-only journal for your child that you write in each year, or have a new journal to start each year. Have family members write or draw special messages in the journal for the birthday child. Wrap it up to be opened with the birthday presents each year.

- Save the newspaper from your child's birthday each year to share at some later date.

- Ask the birthday guests to autograph the tablecloth; make sure they include the date. Embroider the autographs or have the writers use colored pens. Use the tablecloth each year, adding new names and telling stories of those who came before. Or have guests sign a white bed sheet that can be made into a quilt.

- Light a large, decorative candle at each birthday party; let the candle burn for as many minutes as your child's age.

- Select a special plate your child uses each year at the birthday party. You can buy a special plate or use a setting from your good china.

- Transfer all the notes you've written to your child over the year into the birthday book. Include the year's best photographs, and tell stories of your child's year.

- Select a month in which there are no family birthdays, and have an "unbirthday" party with "unbirthday" presents for all (unwrapped, of course). Enjoy "unbirthday" cake, games, and songs.

- Decorate a birthday tablecloth each year with your child's handprint and the date. Or make handprints on a wall, a piece of fabric, or a pillowcase. It's a great way for the whole family to watch your child grow.

- Use small, colorful letter magnets to make a birthday sign on the refrigerator. Spell out *Happy Birthday,* your child's name, and the date. Add a photo of the guest of honor to complete the sign!

- Have older children cut their own birthday cake. After the candles are blown out, use a plastic fork to make dotted lines as a cutting guide on the frosting.

- Take photos of your children on their birthday with the number of the birthday written on a large balloon included in the photo. (The name and date can be added, too.)

- Photograph each guest with the birthday child holding the opened gift. You'll have a record of who gave what as well as a photo to use in a thank-you note. (Order two sets when having film developed.)

- For more birthday tips, games, and recipes, check out my *Birthday Parties: Best Party Tips and Ideas* (Book Peddlers, 800-255-3379).

Holiday Myth and Magic

Parents often struggle with the idea of perpetuating stories of Santa, the Easter Bunny, and even the Tooth Fairy. Yet most parents feel these stories are part of the magic of childhood, and part of what made their own childhood special. They're ways of continuing beautiful traditions and creating powerful memories.

- Let Santa be the one who leaves gifts that Mom and Dad would never buy.

- Tell older children who discover the "truth" behind holiday heroes to help keep the secret from younger children. Keeping the secret is a "coming of age" ritual that helps older children feel grown-up.

- Make stencils of a Santa footprint for Christmas and a bunny footprint for Easter. Use the stencils to create magical footprints on your carpet with baking soda. (It vacuums up easily.) Sprinkle a little baking soda around to add to the wonderment of the holiday.

- Use a little glitter under your child's pillow to show signs of the tooth fairy's visit. (See pages 90–91 for additional ideas.)

Gift-Giving Holidays

- Begin the gift-giving season by having your kids look through catalogs and mark the items they like. It's a good way to find out what your kids want.

- Take your children to a toy store and let them pick out a toy to give to a less fortunate child, to teach them the joy of giving as well as receiving.

- Have your children wrap gifts with their artwork.

- Use extra family photos as gift tags.

- Let your kids choose a toy to give to their grandparents on each gift-giving holiday. The toys remain at the grandparents' home as a permanent entertainment source during visits.

- Let your children wake up Christmas morning with a cherry-red lipstick kiss from Santa imprinted on their foreheads.

- Give each child a Christmas tree ornament every year. Store the ornaments separately, and save them as a treasured collection.

- Save special or outgrown toys to use as Christmas ornaments.

- Give your child certain types of gifts each year to make opening presents exciting: something to read, something to eat, something to play with outside, something snuggly to wear, something soft to take to bed, and so on. Or give only three types of gifts (as in Christian tradition): something special from Mom and Dad, something the child wants, and something needed.

• Take a photo of your child appreciating a gift given by a relative or friend, and send it as a thank-you note to the gift giver.

Hiding Holiday Gifts

It helps to be creative, if not downright crafty, when it comes to hiding all those packages at gift-giving time. There are pros and cons of wrapping presents as you go. The biggest problem of prewrapping is remembering what you've wrapped. The advantage is that, if discovered, the gift remains a surprise. So where to stash them? Try:

• In large trash bags in the attic or basement or under your bed

• In the garage under blankets or in large lawn bags

• In seldom opened cabinets such as a wet bar

• In the linen closet

• In the trunk of your car

• In your neighbor's basement or garage

Keeping Records

The most important official record that parents must keep is their child's birth certificate. It's important to make sure the certificate is made out correctly. Keep it in a safe place, because you may need it when your child starts school, applies for a license or passport, and so forth. Many parents store one certified copy in a safe deposit box and keep others at home for use as needed.

Other records are important for your child's medical history. And still others (diaries, tapes, and photos) provide pleasant memories for a lifetime.

Medical and Legal Records

Some parents keep a notebook containing a child's medical, legal, and school records. If advice and comments from doctors, dentists, and teachers are included, the notebook can help keep track of any recurring problems a child may have.

- Use the back of a copy of your child's birth certificate to record childhood diseases and their dates of occurrence.

- Use index cards to keep track of your child's medical history, including illnesses, dates of vaccinations, and other information. The cards can go with your child to camp or school and can be maintained for a lifetime.

- Carry a few index cards in your purse or wallet so you can make notes at your child's doctor's office or school. Transfer the notes to your child's permanent record at your leisure.

Written Records

- Use a calendar for a baby record book if you don't want to keep a regular one. Or buy a baby record book in calendar format. Use a new calendar each year to record developmental milestones and special moments from your child's day.

- Keep a pad and pencil handy to note your child's milestones. Enter them in the official baby book when you have time. This way you won't have to worry about forgetting things.

- Write down your children's funniest or most memorable lines from childhood. You'll enjoy reading them when your kids are older; plus, they'll make a lasting keepsake.

- Start a family diary in a three-ring binder. Add to it as often as possible (family jokes, a holiday letter, vacation notes, and so on).

- Mark your child's height on a piece of transparent tape attached to a wall or door frame. Indicate your child's name, the date, and the height in inches. Do this at the same time each year, removing last year's marker and saving it in your child's scrapbook.

Spoken Records

Audiotape recorders are valuable tools, even if we do hate hearing our voices on tape. Children usually love recording themselves right from the start.

- Consider taping "talks" you have with your baby during feeding and diaper changes. Review the day's events and your baby's progress and accomplishments. Save the tapes for your child to listen to in the future.

- Tape-record all kinds of family events, from ordinary dinner table conversations to family meetings and holiday celebrations.

- Record your child telling a favorite story at various ages. The changes in your child's voice and vocabulary will amaze you both, and you'll have a precious record of your child's development.

Photographic and Other Visual Records

Get good photos by moving in close and snapping quickly. (Babies and little children don't stay still for long.) Take lots of shots to make sure you get some good ones. Keep backgrounds simple and uncluttered, and get down to your child's eye level.

- Tell your child to show you her teeth or say "Cookie" to capture that winning smile.

- Photograph a restless child by giving her a piece of transparent tape as a playful distraction. It won't show up in the photo.

- Have your child hold the family pet or a favorite toy if she's embarrassed at photo time.

- Photograph or videotape your child getting on the bus or walking toward the front door on the first day of school.

- Make stick puppets from extra photos of family members. Cut out the photo, glue it to a piece of poster board, and attach it to a Popsicle stick.

- Take a semiannual photo of your child standing by a familiar piece of furniture or beside a parent whose hand rests on your child's head. Each half-year's growth will show up dramatically.

- Make photocopies of your child's hands periodically.

- Trace your child's silhouette from a shadow every year or so.

- Make photo sharing less expensive by using photocopies (either color or black and white). Or scan photos and send them electronically.

- Photocopy family photos in black and white, and staple them together to make a personalized coloring book for your child.

- Preserve your baby's first shoes by filling them with plaster of Paris and spraying them with gold, silver, or bronze paint. Take a photo of the shoes for posterity.

Lights, Camera, Action!

Video and digital cameras that allow replay on TVs and computer screens are now so accessible and easy to use that everyone seems to be making family documentaries. If you can't afford to own one, consider renting or borrowing one for special occasions. Moving pictures capture us in a very special way.

- Remember that video cameras record sound along with pictures. Try to do your directing before you start recording.

- You can never pan too slowly.

- Short, frequent use of the camera will give you a better history than overly long footage of just a few family events.

- No one likes being filmed, but everyone likes looking back on themselves. Knowing this, find a middle ground of assertiveness in your filmmaking.

- Sharing videos or digital photos with long-distance relatives is always appreciated.

- Consider designating one VCR cassette or computer disk for each child's birthday, for special holidays, and so on. Use it for only that event, to make finding special events much easier. As your children grow up, you can provide an annual history of their birthday parties for them to share with their friends.

Chapter 7

Families on the Go

Today's families are part of a highly mobile society. They go out to work and play and shop, they travel on vacations, and many move every year. Busy parents try to make each trip as enjoyable, convenient, and safe as possible for their kids and themselves.

Errands

Start out with a list of places to go and things to do, and plan the best route to make your trip as efficient as possible. Pile library books, shopping lists, and other supplies in a special place near the door where you won't forget them.

Shopping with a small child or with several children is no easy task. Many parents try to shop alone for big grocery orders, and some say they're able to save sitters' fees because of the careful comparison shopping they're able to do without kids along. For older children, though, a trip to the store can be a learning experience in both nutrition and economy.

Making Shopping Easier

• Get yourself dressed first (in cold weather) to avoid setting out with an overheated baby or toddler.

• Keep a few disposable diapers in your glove compartment, just in case. Tuck a packaged towelette and a plastic bag inside each diaper to make cleanup and disposal easier. Keep extra diapers and wipes at Grandma's house, too, for unplanned visits.

- Hook some large safety pins on your key chain; you might need them for diapers or quick clothing pinups.

- Change your baby on a blanket in the open trunk or hatchback of a car, or on the tailgate of a station wagon or SUV, instead of crouching uncomfortably in the back seat.

- Use an adult's belt or an elastic stretch belt as a shopping cart safety belt if the cart doesn't have one.

- If your baby is too small to sit in the grocery cart, try sitting him in one of the little carry-along shopping baskets provided. Set the basket in the child seat of the shopping cart. Or choose a cart with a special baby seat. Or keep your baby in an infant seat placed inside the cart.

- Keep a restless older child entertained with a long strip of transparent tape on his finger. If you don't have any in your purse, ask a store worker or cashier for a piece.

- Carry small toys and a pacifier in your purse or pocket, and attach them securely to the shopping cart with shower curtain rings or a short piece of yarn or elastic. (Make sure the yarn or elastic isn't long enough to fit around your baby's neck.) Attach rattles and other small toys to stroller handles and car seats the same way. Try this on the highchair, too, so your baby can fish for toys. Stuffed animals can wear cheap cat collars with yarn leashes.

- Cover your shopping cart handle with a two-foot length of plastic tubing or a shower rod cover to protect your teething infant, or make a terry cloth handle wrap with Velcro so you don't have to worry about germs.

- Give your kids something to eat, since the sight of food sometimes begets a desire for it. Bring a snack or lunch, or buy something nutritious at the store.

- Avoid the "Can I have this?" question by giving your child one dollar to spend. Deciding what to buy will keep him occupied.

- Invest in a fold-up potty seat adapter for a toilet-trained (or almost toilet-trained) child. It turns any adult toilet into a comfortable toilet for a child. (Available in stores, catalogues, and by calling 800-255-3379.)

Keeping Tabs on Kids

Don't attach your child's name to clothing in an obvious or clearly visible way, since a lost child is apt to respond positively to anyone who knows her name, and some strangers are dangerous. In the same vein, avoid clothes or jewelry that would identify your child by name to a stranger. A good alternative is an ID bracelet. Write your child's name and other important information on the blank underside of an attractive strip of paper. Use clear tape to laminate both sides, and tape it around your child's wrist. It's waterproof, disposable, and excellent protection for wandering children.

- Attach a helium balloon to your child's wrist, and have her "pump" it if she gets lost. Personalize the balloon by drawing a design, if you like.

- Buy two balloons (one for each hand) to prevent your child from grabbing and handling things.

- Dress your child in bright-colored clothing to make her easier to find in a crowd. (A red hat will do!)

- Have a special family whistle or tune your children can use to locate you if you get separated in a crowd.

Involving Your Kids in Shopping

- Share a handful of box tops or coupons for your child to match up with products you intend to buy. Or make up a grocery list in pictures for your child to follow as you follow your written list.

- Take advantage of the opportunity to teach your child about nutrition, explaining why you buy certain items and not others. If your child wants you to buy something unhealthy, say, "No, because I love you, and I want you to grow up to be strong and healthy."

- When you give your child permission for a major purchase, put the money in an envelope for a week. If your child still wants it after waiting a week, buy it. Children's interests change quickly, and this helps avoid impulse buying.

City Travel with Kids

- Set your baby's infant seat in the stroller if your child isn't old enough to sit up.

- Use a baby harness or toddler wrist leash if your toddler is tired of the stroller. Embroider it or sew on appliqués to make it look more personalized and less like a leash.

- Take a booster seat in the theater so your older (yet small) child can see the screen without being in your lap. He'll be more comfortable, too. When the booster seat is outgrown for home use, keep it in your car for spur-of-the-moment movie outings.

- Ride the subway in the front or back of the train so your kids can watch the tracks racing by. Let your kids try to figure out which stop is theirs so they can learn their way around. Let them sit a few seats away and pretend they're traveling alone, if they want to. It will make them feel grown-up, and they may pay closer attention to the route.

Trips

Adults may be able to throw a few things into a bag and dash off, but not when kids are coming along. Traveling with babies six months or younger is fairly easy, since they take long naps and don't move around much. With older children, you need to plan carefully.

Packing

It's hard to travel light with children. Clothing, food, and toys take lots of space, but imaginative packing pays off. A backpack and/or umbrella stroller is well worth the space taken up. Older children enjoy selecting and packing the things they want to bring. You'll need to set limits as to types, sizes, and number of toys allowed. Take only what fits in your child's backpack or suitcase.

- Simplify the project by designating specific bags for specific items ("Susie's clothes," for example, or a nighttime suitcase for the whole family). Put children's clothing on top for easy access if you're sharing suitcases.

- Use duffel bags for kids' clothes and toys. They fit more easily into the car, trunk, or overhead compartment on a plane. A nylon duffel bag can be used for wet or soiled diapers, since it's washable. It's also good for wet clothes and bathing suits.

- Save space by bringing inflatable toys. When not in use, they can be deflated and tucked away.

- Pack disposable diapers in the corners of suitcases to save the space a big bag or box would take.

- Let your baby's quilt double as a changing pad. Slip it in a pillowcase and tie a ribbon around it for easy transport.

- Pack several large plastic bags. They can be used for soiled laundry and to protect the sheets of the occasional bed-wetter. Or bring a bath rug with rubber backing to lay down on top of a sheet. It rolls up easily for travel.

- Use a see-through lingerie case with zippered pockets and a hanger for small items for babies and parents. The bag is easily moved and hung, and the contents are visible.

- Pack a few of your baby's things to make strange surroundings seem more familiar (a crib sheet or receiving blanket, a few toys, a doll or stuffed animal, and so on).

- Attach name tags to special pillows, blankets, and toys so they can be returned if forgotten.

- Keep any needed medication with you instead of in your luggage. Take your medical information and phone numbers with you, too, just in case.

Little Things That Can Make a Big Difference

- Bring a fanny pack (or belt pack) for carrying small items, so you'll have both hands available for your child and won't have to carry a purse.

- Take along a nightlight to reassure children who wake up in the night in a strange room.

- Bring your baby monitor. It can be helpful at a relative's home or in a hotel when you want to keep tabs on your sleeping baby.

- Take along a few outlet covers and cabinet door locks if you'll be staying in places that aren't childproofed.

- Keep first-aid items and baby wipes in a glove compartment or in a purse, fanny pack, or carryon bag.

Comfort in the Car

Even if you're traveling in a large vehicle with plenty of room, you'll want to keep things organized and accessible.

- Make a slipcover to hang over the front seat of the car, with several pockets in the back for books, games, and toys. A shoe bag with several pockets is perfect for organizing travel gear.

- Stuff a pillowcase with bulky, cold-weather clothing. You'll have a pillow for napping, and the clothing will be in one place.

- Consider renting a crib or other needed equipment after arriving at your destination. Check out diaper services, too! You don't have to *bring* everything!

Peace in the Car

Parents who travel a lot are used to children's initial excitement and restlessness in the car. Kids usually settle down after an hour or so, once territories and rules have been defined. Don't start the car until everyone's buckled in. If a child unbuckles while you're driving, pull off to the side and say, "The car will not move unless your seat belt is buckled." Traveling with kids just takes longer, so incorporate that into your travel schedule.

- Travel at night, or get an early start so your children will sleep in the car. But don't encourage so much sleep that you have well-rested kids at night when you're ready to sleep.

- Put a small suitcase or box between two children in the back seat, to define their territories. Or put a firm diaper bag filled with small toys and books between two toddlers in car seats, to keep them entertained and occupied. (Stash some favorite toys and books in the bag several days before you leave, so they'll have more appeal.)

- Change seating arrangements occasionally. One adult in the back seat for all or half of a trip usually makes for a pleasant journey.

- Stop periodically to run and play with your kids. The break will be good for everybody. Pack a bottle of bubbles or a package of balloons in the glove compartment. Stash a Frisbee, ball, or jump rope under a seat.

- Give your kids a five-minute warning before you stop, so they can put on their shoes and coats, if necessary.

- Announce a treat for the end of the day so everyone will have something to look forward to (a swim in the pool, dinner at a favorite restaurant, and so on).

- Take along headphones for kids—and earplugs for adults!

For Fussy Travelers

- Bring out a new toy or snack occasionally.
- Keep the radio on with lively music.
- Bring tapes or CDs and do lots of singing.
- Stop every hour or two.
- Praise positive behavior.
- Keep trips short if your child's an unhappy camper.
- Invest in a TV/VCR for your car to keep kids entertained.

Back Seat Bickering

- Stop the car and pull over when fighting begins, and don't go again until it ends. Get out of the car, if necessary, until your kids have quieted down.
- Let kids know that fighting endangers everyone in the car. Consider deducting something from their allowance or withholding privileges.
- Talk to your older kids before you leave, and ask them how fighting should be handled. Use their usable suggestions.
- Use money as an incentive for kids old enough to be swayed by cash. Add an amount (a quarter or whatever) to each child's spending account for each hour without an incident; deduct the same amount for bickering. Settle up each day.

Food in the Car

Avoid spill disasters by carrying an extra set of clothing for each child and a plastic bag for soiled clothes. It's also a good idea to cover the back seat with a sheet or cotton blanket; just shake out the crumbs at rest stops. Keep baby wipes or packaged towelettes handy, and bring along a squeezable water bottle with a little liquid soap added. You can always use windshield wiper fluid as a last resort.

- Use a small cooler to keep baby food warm or cold. Tape the baby spoon to one of the jars.

- Use a cardboard six-pack carton when traveling. Each compartment can hold a little sack of pretzels, candy, napkins, or juice; plus it's easy to carry.

- See "The Business of Bottles" (page 9) for ideas about baby bottles.

- Pack instant baby cereal in separate small plastic bags or containers with powdered milk or formula. Add warm water from a Thermos or the hot tap of a sink when you're ready to feed your baby. Use a cooler for frozen baby food cubes or "plops" (for babies) and homemade juice Popsicles (for older kids).

- Carry a supply of small paper plates or coffee filters with little slits in the center. Put the sticks of Popsicles or ice-cream bars through the slits, and there'll be less mess on car seats and fingers.

- Hang a bagel on a string tied around the arm of the car seat. There won't be many crumbs, and it won't fall on the floor. Make sure the string isn't so long that it can wrap around your child's neck.

- Cut sandwiches in different shapes for easy identification: triangles for those with mustard, rectangles for those with mayonnaise, and so on.

- Fill several small plastic bags with an assortment of treats such as raisins, dry cereal, and sunflower seeds. Bring them out when spirits need reviving.

- Take along a box of crackers and a tube of squirt cheese. The adult who's not driving can decorate the crackers.

- Avoid taking very salty foods in the car; they inspire lots of drinking—and lots of rest stops.

Drinks in the Car

- Carry a Thermos of cold water; it quenches thirst best. Add a slice of lemon or a little lemon juice for flavor.

- Make crisscross slits in a baby bottle nipple, invert, and secure with the cap and cover on the plastic baby bottle. When your toddler needs a drink, remove the cover, fill it with your toddler's favorite beverage, and insert a straw. No spills!

- Put liquids in well-washed plastic lemon or lime juice dispensers. (Remove the inserts with a sharp pointed object, replace after filling, and screw the caps back on.) If you freeze them before you leave, the drinks will stay cool as they melt.

- Satisfy both thirst and hunger with grapes. Older kids may prefer frozen grapes. (Always cut them in half for toddlers.) Oranges serve the same purpose, but they're messier.

- Freeze a large or small plastic container half full of water. When you're ready to go, fill the rest of the container with water for a long-lasting, cold thirst quencher.

- Take a few cloth diapers or a roll of paper towels along to mop up spills. Absorbency is the key.

- Keep flexible straws in your purse. They make it easier for children to drink from cups in a restaurant or car seat.

- Give your child a plastic sports bottle with a straw for a nonspillable drink. Or use bottles with pop-up tops.

- Refill pint-size plastic juice bottles with water or juice. They're great for short outings, and they save the cost of small boxed drinks.

Eating in Restaurants

- Assemble a "restaurant kit" with children's utensils, snacks, baby wipes, a highchair strap or belt, small toys, and a bib (or a small plastic clothespin, diaper pin, or sweater guard to snap a napkin around your child's neck). Make restaurant personnel happy by bringing a piece of newspaper to spread out under the highchair. Bring a cheap and easy booster seat (a couple of old catalogs wrapped in Contact paper or duct tape) in case the restaurant doesn't have one.

- Let kids drink with straws. They're fun and they help prevent spills. Cutting them in half or partway makes handling easier.

- Get in the habit of carrying small pads of paper and colored pencils or washable markers in your bag. They come in handy at restaurants, doctors' offices, and other places where you must wait. Also consider stickers, small books, pipe cleaners, and special toys that are used only in these situations.

- Ask an attendant for a take-out cup with a lid. Put a straw through the slit to prevent spills.

- Walk around outdoors with an impatient toddler while you're waiting for food to be served. Or let your child play with (not eat) ice cubes on the highchair tray, or provide paper napkins or straws.

- Order food with take-out potential, and ask the server which dishes take the least amount of time to serve. Have baskets of bread brought to the table quickly, if possible.

- Order a pot of hot water and extra napkins for general cleanup and for washing a highchair tray that wasn't thoroughly cleaned the last time.

Toys to Take Along

- Secure a nonbreakable crib mirror to the back of a front seat so your child can be entertained while sitting in a car seat.

- Before embarking on a long car trip, wrap a variety of small personalized gifts for your child to open at predetermined times. Be careful not to buy gifts that would be too noisy (whistles) or messy (paint by numbers) in the car.

- Bring a plastic dishpan to hold your toddler's favorite toys and books. Set it beside the car seat for a self-service library.

- Keep a stuffed animal buckled into your child's empty car seat. It provides an instant toy for car trips, plus it sets a good example.

- Keep most of your child's toys in the trunk or cargo hatch. Bring out a few items after each rest stop, and return others to the trunk.

- Tie toys to your child's car seat with short strings so you won't have to pick them up constantly.

- Let your children fill school lunch boxes with small toys (but not *so* small that they'll get lost in the car).

- Put small toys in a hanging shoe bag with many pockets. Keep it rolled up in the car, and let it hang on a door in the hotel room to keep toys available and off the floor.

- Wrap some favorite toys and a few new ones with plenty of string and tape, to keep your child busy with unwrapping. (You'll have some litter to clean up, though.)

Activities in the Car

Check your local library for books on games to play and songs to sing in the car. Keep a list of favorite songs and games in the glove compartment so you won't forget them when you suddenly need a diversion.

- Tape greeting cards, magazine pictures, even a swatch of your baby's wallpaper to the back of the front seat, so your child will have something interesting to look at.

- Draw faces on your child's fingers or hands (or your own) with washable markers. Enjoy puppet "conversations" or stories!

- Make a simple map even small children can follow as you drive. Indicate landmarks and stops along the way.

- Put everyone's imagination to the test by "seeing things" in cloud formations.

- Store colored pencils, markers, and coloring books in a metal cake pan with a sliding cover. (Crayons melt in the summer heat.) The closed top provides a work surface. Avoid scissors—their sharp points may prove dangerous in case of a sudden stop.

- Buy magnetized games, or glue pieces of Velcro to board games and playing pieces to keep small parts from getting lost. Put dice in a clear plastic jar (to be shaken) rather than having your kids roll them and potentially lose them.

- Take along a big catalog for your children to look at.

- Buy a small photo album and fill it with photos of family and friends to amuse your children. Update it regularly.

- Buy postcards at your favorite places while traveling. Write down the day's activities on the back of the cards. Put them in a scrapbook you've brought along, or mail them to your home address.

- Play tapes you've made of favorite stories and songs, or use tapes you've checked out from the library.

Distractions That Can Save the Day

- Arrange Cheerios in a design on a highchair or car seat tray, or bring a string so they can be strung into a necklace.

- Act silly. Make funny faces, teach pig Latin, put on a red clown nose, and so on. A quick change to silliness can change things from frantic to fun.

- Have your kids count your money in your purse or wallet, or let them "read" and talk about what they see on coins and paper money.

- Use your imagination. Ask your kids what they think it looks like on the moon. Make up a story about the person across the room. Play, "I spy something…" and have your children try to guess what it is. (For younger children, make it easier by narrowing the focus, such as, "I spy something blue.") Use your finger to draw a letter or number on your child's back; have your child try to guess what it is.

Traveling by Plane

Babies under two travel free, but you must inform the airline that you're traveling with a baby. Check with the airline or your travel agent to find out what flights are least crowded, so you can get an extra seat for your baby. (The idea of traveling at night, so the kids will sleep, doesn't necessarily apply to air travel.)

- Request window and aisle seats in a three-row section, and hope that the middle seat won't be taken.

- Try to board the plane with a freshly diapered baby. There's little room for changing in an airplane restroom. Double-diapering or inserting a sanitary napkin inside the disposable can be helpful. Carry a backpack or a soft cloth diaper bag with a shoulder strap, instead of a bulkier "boxy" bag. Fill it with more diapers than you think you'll need, in case you get stranded without luggage. Motion sickness bags are good for soiled diapers, but don't leave filled ones at your seat. Ask a flight attendant to take care of them.

- Board as early as you can. Get a blanket and pillow from the overhead rack as you're being seated.

- Carry a small infant in a front pack to keep your hands free. Some feel the front pack is safest for takeoff and landing. Make sure the seat belt is over *your* pelvis, not your baby's.

- Nurse your baby, or give a bottle or pacifier at takeoff and landing to reduce pressure in your baby's ears. Have gum or hard candy available for older children. Blowing up a balloon often helps older children, too. Teach children to swallow, chew, and yawn to open Eustachian tubes. Make a game of facial motions for your baby. Even crying can equalize pressure and reduce pain. This is especially important if your child has a cold or allergies.

- Most car seats can now be taken on board an airplane. Check with your airline to make sure yours is acceptable. Remember that you'll be paying for another seat if your child is under two and you want to be assured of an extra seat.

- Car seats and strollers can be checked at the entry ramp or stairway before boarding.

- Let an older child carry things in a backpack.

- Bring some new toys and books (small, of course) and hand them out one at a time. A deck of cards is good. A miniature

Magna Doodle works well, too. Make sure not to bring anything that could be dangerous if your child were to throw it.

- Don't rush as you're leaving the plane. Seasoned air travelers say leaving last is best, unless you're right up front.

Eating on the Plane

- Request a child's plate or fruit plate at least two days before departing, to ensure appropriate finger foods.

- Check with a flight attendant to find out the best time to get help with warming a bottle or changing your baby.

- Bring some food from home for your child. Airplane snacks are often nuts or crunchy things babies shouldn't eat, and you'll have something in case of delays. Cheerios are a good crumb-free snack.

- Avoid cola drinks for children. Two or three have as much caffeine as a cup of coffee, and they'll make it hard for your child to sit still. They're also a diuretic.

- Don't drink a hot beverage while your child is active or in your lap. If it spills, you can scald your child.

Enjoying the Outdoors

It's important to remember that children, even responsible preschoolers, must be watched constantly and carefully when you're in the woods or near water. Possibilities for fun and learning are abundant, however. Rainy-day puddles are as exciting as sunsets and wildlife.

Camping with Kids

Roughing it with small children is not for everyone. If you're not sure you can handle it, choose a campground with bathrooms, laundry facilities, and a general store for your first outing. You may feel safer if your campsite isn't near a road, lake, or stream. As with any trip, enjoy each moment on its own terms; original plans and destinations sometimes have to be modified.

Before the Camping Trip

• Stage a practice run in your backyard. You can test all your equipment and accustom your child to the experience.

• Pack rain gear, boots, and jackets no matter what the weather report says. Make washability a priority for camping clothes, and keep layering in mind when selecting items.

• Pack some clothing and gear in plastic pails you can use for dishwashing, hand laundry, and grooming. A large plastic container with a lid makes a great mini laundry tub for little items. Just add a little soap, put on the lid, and shake. (Shaking is more efficient than swishing.)

• Avoid the odors of damp, soiled clothing by packing fabric softener sheets in laundry bags.

• Take along a backpack carrier for hiking with a young child, but build up your carrying time before your trip. Pack a small mirror you can use as a rear view mirror while you're hiking.

• Make up a nature box that includes books on birds, rocks, and trees. Also include plastic bags, jars, and boxes for storing things. Give your child collecting assignments such as three leaves, five rocks, two pinecones, and so on.

• Pack a good first-aid book and kit containing supplies for insect bites, sunburn, cuts, bruises, fever, and so on. Include a tweezers for splinters.

• Consider bringing your own drinking water, a water filter, or water-purification tablets if you don't trust the water at the campground. You *don't* want your child to get diarrhea!

On the Camping Trip

- Use empty plastic bread bags for soiled diapers and other wet items.

- Line a five-gallon, plastic, lidded bucket with a plastic bag, fill it with clean clothes, and use it as a suitcase. Lift the bag to place dirty clothes underneath. Buckets are waterproof and can double as stools. (Be careful with plastic bags around young children.)

- Use your empty cooler as a bathtub. (Keep an eye on your child at all times!)

- Use a small, inflatable wading pool as a bathtub. When dry, you can add a quilt or pad and use it as a crib or playpen. This works well at the beach, too.

- Always travel with food and drink in the car, even if you plan to buy most of your supplies at the campground, so you're prepared for the unexpected.

- Create a nature bracelet by loosely wrapping a strip of transparent tape around your child's wrist, sticky side up. Small treasures can be stuck to the bracelet when your child is out exploring.

- Keep Avon's Skin-So-Soft towelettes in your baby bag to use whenever mosquitoes are biting. (Canned spray repellents should not be used on babies.) Or use a citric repellent that's safe for babies.

At the Beach

- Remember that children burn much more easily than adults. Put hats on small children, and use a good sun block on their skin. Don't spray lotion on children. Spray it on your hand, and then apply it to your child's face.

- Use a big sheet instead of a blanket or towel for children to sit on. It's cooler, sand shakes off easily, and it folds neatly and compactly for transport. An inflatable pool is also a good way to keep your baby and baby toys off the sand.

- Put beach gear into a plastic sled or laundry basket to pull across the sand.

- Carry beach toys in a mesh bag or plastic laundry basket you can dunk in the water for a quick rinse at the end of the day.

- Prop up your baby in a plastic laundry basket lined with towels to keep her safe and out of the sand.

- Use a round toothbrush holder to carry a paring knife or baby spoon when traveling to a picnic or the beach.

- Mark your beach toys, since yours will probably look like everyone else's. Red nail polish works well.

- Put large jar lids under the legs of a playpen to keep it from sinking into the sand. (This works well in your yard at home, too.)

- Turn a playpen upside down over a blanket or sheet to keep the hot sun off your child and your child off the hot sand. You can also stretch a fitted crib sheet over the corners of a playpen to protect your child from the sun. Or open a large umbrella on a blanket.

- Remove diapers before taking your baby in the water. They absorb too much water and become very heavy, so your baby loses natural buoyancy. Or use disposable swim diapers. (They're required for a pool!)

- Fill a pail with water before leaving the beach, and have your children dip their feet in it before getting in the car.

- Sprinkle baby powder over your children's sandy arms and legs. Brush off powder and sand together.

- Remove sand from chairs, buckets, shovels, and even feet by using a clean, broad paintbrush. Keep it in your trunk.

- Remove sand and dirt from pant cuffs using the sweeper attachment of your vacuum cleaner.

Moving

Parents who have moved a lot say they try not to let a move disrupt their children's sense of security. You can help ease the transition by involving your children as much as possible, by letting them be the first to know about the move, and by sharing your enthusiasm and excitement.

Before You Move

- If you're staying in town, take the children to see the new house or apartment, at least from the outside. Show them the points of interest in the neighborhood. If possible, let them meet and talk with children who live in the neighborhood. If you're moving out of town, try to get photos of the new home and local landmarks.

- Spend some relaxed family time in your new home before you move, if you can. Hang a few photos and bring in some familiar objects and toys to bridge the gap between old and new.

- If some of your children's things will be sold, let them decide which ones, if possible. Earmark the money for new toys in the new home.

- Let your kids pack their possessions as you pack yours, to give them a feeling of helping. Let them decorate their own boxes so they'll know which things they want to unpack first.

- Give yourself a break (and save time and work) by having a sitter play with your kids while you pack.

- Pack sheets and a blanket with each mattress so you'll have beds to sleep in during the unpacking.

- Load children's furniture and boxes last, so they come off first.

The New Environment

The experience of moving out of one home and into another can be traumatic for both children and adults, but it can also be fun and exciting. Some parents believe it's best to have kids out of the house at both ends of a move, if possible. Dismantling rooms and setting up new ones is much easier with kids out of the way. Other parents recommend involving children as much as possible to create a special family experience.

- Nurse your baby through your move, and plan to wean only after you're settled. Delay toilet training, too.

- Set up your child's room first.

- Find a sitter to play with your children while you unpack. Besides being able to settle in more easily, you'll have a chance to observe and supervise the new sitter.

- Have a picnic in the new house for the first meal, including favorite easy foods or sandwiches. Try to make it special amid the boxes and confusion. Talk about how things will be as the furniture gets settled, and remind your kids that they may never be able to eat in the center of the dining room floor again.

- Pay kids a penny (or more) for each moving sticker they remove from a piece of furniture.

- Ask a friend or relative to send your child a welcoming post-card or letter to the new address, so it'll be waiting when you get there.

Chapter 8

Child's Play

Child's play is learning, and many who have studied child development say that the more imaginative the play, the more a child learns. Most parents have seen a child become more fascinated with the box a toy comes in than the toy itself. This is not to say that you shouldn't buy toys, but to suggest that the fun and learning of play can depend upon what's at hand as well.

Daycare

- Keep a small notebook to exchange with your daycare provider as you drop off and pick up your kids. Share notes back and forth to keep each other up to date. Even if it's only one sentence or a short affirmation, it's a good habit to develop.

- Attach a luggage tag to your child's diaper bag or backpack. Include parents' work numbers, other vital names and numbers, and pertinent home information.

- Slow down. Children usually do better when their pickup isn't rushed. They may want to show you an accomplishment or have you meet a new friend.

- Prepare your child for a new daycare by stopping by early the first few times (before most of the other children arrive) and letting her check out the toys. Your child will probably be eager to return. Take a photo of your child with her new daycare provider, and post it on your refrigerator at home.

- Tape your child's photo to her bottle or sippy cup so it won't be confused with another child's.

- Send a camera to your child's preschool, and have the teacher, if willing, take photos over the course of the day. Make an album or poster with the photos so you and your child can use them to talk about the day's events.

- Make private home child care more affordable by sharing one childcare provider between two families.

Good-Bye Rituals

It's reasonable for a child to be apprehensive about separating from a parent in a new situation. These transitions often take a few weeks to complete. Tears and clingy behavior are normal. Don't dismiss your child's fears, but don't let a meltdown control you either. Let your preschooler know that you are going. Ideally, use a week for a transition. (Stay less time each day, and shorten your good-bye time as your child eases in to the new environment.)

- Remind your child of when you (or someone else) will pick him up.

- Establish a good-bye ritual such as a hug, a goodbye wave, or a funny face from the doorstep or window.

- Let an older child be part of the leave-taking process. Ask for his opinions.

- Plant a big red lipstick kiss on your child's arm, palm, or tummy. Your child can look at the kiss whenever a feeling of loneliness or missing Mom or Dad surfaces.

Seasonal Fun

A climate like that of the South Sea Islands often seems like a dream come true to parents of active kids: warm weather year round...no mittens, caps, scarves, or jackets. Hardy souls in the North, though, enjoy the change between summer and winter.

Warm-Weather Specials

- Attach a special baby swing to the swing set so all your kids can swing together.

- Put an old rubber doormat or a piece of indoor-outdoor carpeting under the swing to protect shoes and to keep some of the dirt outdoors.

- Fill a flour shaker with cornstarch or flour, and let your kids sprinkle everything in sight outdoors. The first shower will clean it all up.

- Let your kids draw on the sidewalk with white or colored chalk. Rain or a hose will erase the artwork.

- Tape newspaper down on a driveway, and let your kids paint on it using tempera paint mixed with some liquid soap.

- Make a sandbox by setting an old tractor tire on the ground and filling it about half full with sand. There's plenty of seating space all around. Or use an old plastic swimming pool that no longer holds water. Sink it into the ground, punch a few holes in the bottom, and fill it with sand (the coarse kind, not the fine variety). Or don't bother to sink it.

- Fill your "sandbox" with birdseed instead of sand (assuming your child is old enough to know not to eat it). Add shovels, toys, and a child for a fun afternoon.

- Hang blankets over the clothesline to make a tent. Or set up a real tent for outdoor sleepovers or naps.

- Invert a plastic wading pool over your sandbox to protect it from leaves, cats, and rain. Use a few logs or bricks to hold it down.

- Let your child help you with garden chores. Consider giving one small plot to care for alone. Choose quick-growing plants such as lettuce, beans, radishes, marigolds, or bachelor buttons.

- Take your child to a miniature golf course early in the morning when it's cool. It's a child-size play world.

Water Play

Indoors use an open, empty dishwasher as a platform for some types of water play. Make sure the soap containers are empty and there are no sharp corners your child could get hurt on. To clean up, just close it up! Outdoor play is obviously easier.

- Make a water pistol out of an empty plastic dish detergent bottle or kitchen baster.

- Put a plastic swimming pool at the bottom of the slide on a hot day, and let your kids slide into the water. (Don't buy a pool you can't empty alone!) Stick bathtub appliqués to the bottom to make it less slippery and to repair any holes.

- Fill balloons three-quarters full with water, close them with twist ties so they can be used again, and toss them around the yard.

- Give your child a dishpan of water, add detergent, and let him whip up suds with an eggbeater. Or let your child dip a plastic six-pack holder (ring-like) into the solution and wave it in the air for lots of bubbles.

- Let your child paint the outside of the house with water and a big paintbrush, or add food coloring to the water and let him paint the sidewalk.

- Make a very small hole in the bottom of a can, attach it to your child's tricycle, and fill it with colored water. Have your child ride until the "gas" is gone.

- Fill a coaster wagon with water; then add funnels, a kitchen baster, and an eggbeater for water fun without dirt. If you can stand the mess, a mud hole in the corner of your yard will delight children even more than a sandbox.

- Let your kids wash the car. It may not be uniformly clean, but they'll have fun. Or let them wash their trikes, bikes, or toys.

- Use a kitchen strainer to get rid of grass, bugs, and dirt floating around in the kiddy pool. To protect an inflatable pool from punctures, place it on an inexpensive shower curtain on the ground.

Snowy-Day Specials

- Use an old plastic baby bathtub for a sled. (Punch a hole in the rim and attach a rope.) It won't go too fast, and the sides will keep a small child from falling out.

- Let a toddler use a dustpan for a snow shovel. It's the right size.

- Teach your kids to play a game of chase in the snow. Draw a big circle by shuffling through the snow, and then draw two bisecting lines at right angles to each other. The players can run only on the lines.

- Show your kids how to make snow angels by lying down spread-eagled and moving their arms up and down and their legs together and apart.

- Fill a plastic squeeze or spray bottle with water, and add a few drops of food coloring so your kids can draw on the snow or paint a snowman.

- Put special marks on a large outdoor thermometer to let your children know when they must wear jackets, boots, and other heavy clothing. (Also mark summer temperatures that are warm enough for picnics and water play.)

- Put a coating of petroleum jelly on your kids' cheeks to protect them from frostbite in cold or windy weather.

- Spray fabric protector on mittens to help them stay dry and keep hands warmer.

- Keep your kids' feet warm while ice skating by cutting a slit along the bottom of a large heavy sock and slipping the sock over the ice skate with the blade going through the slit.

Too Cold, Too Hot, or Too Wet to Go Out

Many parents depend on malls, local pet stores, and the like when weather is lousy. Here are some other options:

- Let your kids play with snow in the kitchen sink, or with *lots* of snow in the bathtub. Cover them with raincoats worn backward or outdoor play clothes. (This activity works best at floor-washing time—things might get messy!)

- Help your kids with a little experiment: Bring a bowl of snow inside, and show them what a small amount of water it makes when it melts.

- Make an indoor sandbox out of any sturdy box or dishpan. Fill it with rice or used coffee grounds. (Hasten the drying process in the oven). It's ideal for roads for little cars.

- Let your kids skinny-dip in the bathtub for a while before naptime or bedtime, to get them warm and sleepy.

- Give your kids a chemistry lesson. Dig out some dirty old pennies; mix vinegar and salt together; have your children dip an old cloth into the solution; and let them polish the pennies!

- Make edible play dough: ¼ cup smooth peanut butter, 2 tablespoons honey, 2 tablespoons powdered milk, and enough powdered chocolate drink mix so it's not sticky. Mix until it has a doughy consistency. Mold it into shapes, or roll it out and cut it with cookie cutters.

- Make edible finger paint: one small package instant vanilla pudding mix, and ½ cup water. Mix well. Add food coloring to make different colors, or use chocolate pudding for brown.

- Accumulate small, inexpensive items in a "bored" bag for rainy days. (Keep the bag a secret.) Some things to include are games, books, toys, and small snacks like little cans of fruit, pudding, or juice.

- Go to the public library and check out some arts-and-crafts books or other activity books.

- Glue colored construction paper onto flexible magnets. Cut out a circle, and write the word *circle* on it. Make other shape magnets to display on the refrigerator. Do the same with duplicate family photos or magazine photos.

Indoors and Out

You can buy loads of expensive toys and equipment that are educational and fun for your children to play with, and you can take your children places where they'll learn a lot and have a good time. But you can also supply inexpensive things or "found" items that will provide hours of fun.

Playhouses, Forts, and Such

- Drape an old sheet over a card table to make a playhouse that can be put up and taken down in minutes. Cut or draw windows and doors, and let your kids decorate by drawing flowers, shutters, and bricks with markers.

- Use a large mover's carton or a big box from a household appliance to make a playhouse. Cut doors and windows, and let your children draw curtains, rugs, and pictures inside, and shrubbery, shutters, and a doorbell outside. Remember that large cartons can also be forts, tunnels, trains, and boats. Just use your imagination!

- Create forts out of couch cushions, if you're willing.

- Make a secret hideout by hanging bedspreads, sheets, or blankets over chairs. (Hold them in place with spring clothespins.)

- Use chairs and stools to make train or airplane seats.

- Spread magazines or furniture cushions around the floor to make "rooms" and to use as stepping stones. Or use carpet squares for "magic carpets."

- Put an old mattress on the floor for tumbling and jumping, to save wear and tear on chairs, couches, and beds.

- Make a dollhouse by attaching four same-size boxes together (two up and two down). Cut windows and doors. Give your child scraps of cloth, wallpaper, or carpeting, and let her decorate.

- The puppet theater you buy or make for indoor activities can be used as a lemonade stand in the summer.

Games

- Make a "busy box" for a toddler or infant by attaching various items to a heavy cardboard box (things to spin, a bell to ring, a lock and key, a chain to rattle, knobs, balls, and so on).

- Give an old shower curtain new life. Use a heavy felt-tip pen to design a village full of roads and railroad tracks. Your child can spread it out and play with cars, trucks, and trains.

- Give your toddler a paper-towel tube and a blown-up balloon for a safe, easy baseball game. Tubes also make good tunnels for little cars.

- Make a baseball stand by stacking two tennis ball cans. Kids have as much fun knocking over the cans as they do hitting the ball.

- Paint small, empty juice cans or eight-ounce plastic bottles, and let your child use them for bowling pins.

- Get out a box of old clothes and let your child play dress-up. Use old receiving blankets for capes, skirts, and veils.

- Give your child scraps of wrapping paper, tape, and pieces of ribbon to play birthday party. Have your child wrap his own toys for presents.

- Play dice games with a child who finds dice easier to handle than cards. Make your own dice from gum erasers cut in half and decorated with the usual dots or other symbols.

- Let children who can't manage cards hold them with spring clothespins. Or slip them in the flap slot of a box of aluminum foil or waxed paper.

- Tape strips of masking tape over the corners of boxes of games and puzzles *before* they break. Preserve board games, puzzles, and book covers with Contact paper.

Help Your Child Learn to Be a Good Loser

- Don't let your child beat you *all* the time. Learning disappointment is an important lesson in life.

- Lose board games without cheating by using a handicap system that you devise. In checkers, for example, change sides every three moves. Or make a rule that no player can be more than one captured piece ahead. (After a winner is determined, sometimes it's fun to play until all the pieces are gone.)

- Discuss how well another person did (or did not) handle losing in a situation you've both observed, even one on TV. Let your child know that losing with grace makes one a winner in the end.

- Give your child encouraging comments during the game (such as "Great Move!") to emphasize playing well rather than winning or losing.

- Teach your child appropriate things to say after the game, such as, "Thanks for playing with me," and, "That was a good game even if I lost."

- Praise your child for a loss handled well.

- Be a good role model for your child when you win.

Puzzles

- Glue small, unpainted furniture knobs on puzzle pieces to make them easier for little children to handle. You can paint the knobs to match the pieces.

- Make puzzles by pasting large pictures on heavy cardboard and covering them with clear Contact paper. Cut with a matte knife (or small saw) into several pieces in distinctly different shapes such as stars, triangles, arrows, circles, and squares.

- Keep puzzle pieces from getting hopelessly jumbled by marking the backs of all the pieces of one puzzle with one color, another puzzle with a different color, and so on. They'll be easier to sort if they get inadvertently mixed up.

- Store puzzles separately in self-closing plastic bags.

Things to Unmake and Undo

- Remember that any appliance or gadget on its way to the trash offers fascinating possibilities for unscrewing, opening, taking apart, and even smashing.

- Check out garage sales for broken clocks, record players, or cameras to take apart.

- Let your kids participate in any dismantling project in the house or yard (taking down a wall, digging a garden, breaking up a sidewalk, and so on).

Cleaning and Repairing Toys

- Save yourself work by buying machine-washable stuffed animals and dishwasher-safe plastic toys.

- Put small plastic and rubber toys in a mesh lingerie bag, and place it on the top rack of your dishwasher to clean.

- Clean and deodorize toys by wiping them off with a moist cloth dipped in baking soda.

- Shake unwashable stuffed toys in a bag with generous amounts of cornmeal, baking soda, or cornstarch. Brush out the dry powder, and the dirt will come with it. Or use rug shampoo and a brush.

- Clean cloth dolls by making a paste of soap flakes and water, applying it with a toothbrush, and wiping it off with a damp cloth.

- Paint paper dolls with clear nail polish to keep them from tearing.

- Apply two or three coats of nail polish to pinholes in inflatable toys.

- Soak plastic toys that have gotten out of shape in hot water; then work them back into shape.

- Replace lost checkers by cutting small discs off a wooden broom handle; then sand and paint.

- Give new life to old stuffed animals by removing some or all of the stuffing and turning them into hand puppets.

Arts and Crafts

Don't ask your beginning scribbler or sculptor, "What is it?" Such a question puts a child on the spot. Instead, talk about colors, thickness or thinness of paint, interesting shapes, and so on. Save yourself cleanup trouble by having your child wear an adult's old shirt with shortened sleeves. You'll save yourself more trouble if you have a tiled floor or if you put down a plastic rug runner or piece of linoleum in your child's "creative corner." Vinyl tablecloths make excellent play cloths, too. Covering the work table with an old sheet also makes cleanup easy. Let your child use your old baby nail scissors for cutting. Their blunt tips make them safe yet sharp.

Painting

There are numerous sources of inexpensive paper: rolls of discontinued black-and-white wallpaper, shelf paper, ends of rolls of newsprint from your local newspaper, brown paper bags, even newspaper want-ad pages on which print is dense enough to paint over. Save diaper and shirt boxes with white interiors, and cut them up for painting. Or make a writing or coloring board by covering a piece of cardboard with clear Contact paper. "Erase" with a dampened tissue or paper towel.

You can remove a clear photo-magnetic sheet cover from a photo album and place it over activity book pages such as mazes. Your child can color on the clear sheet with dry erasable marker pens or grease pencils found in office supply shops. This makes activity sheets reuseable because all you need is a tissue to wipe away the colors on the clear sheets.

- Make finger paint for kids with canned milk and food coloring

- Combine shaving cream, shortening, or even instant pudding with food coloring, and let your child paint on the shiny side of freezer paper or on a cookie sheet for gooey fun.

- Mix powdered paint with liquid starch instead of water to get a better consistency for beginning painters.

- Make instant paint by adding a few drops of food coloring to a little liquid starch in a small container.

- Mix a little egg yolk, dry detergent, and food coloring to make a paint that will stick to a shiny surface such as glass, foil, or freezer paper.

- Use wide-mouth lids from large jars to hold just the right amount of paint for brushes. They're also good for sponge painting.

- Use food coloring and brushes to paint marshmallows!

- Avoid trips to the sink for hand cleanup by putting paper towels and a spray bottle filled with water on the work table.

- Buy powdered paints at a teacher's supply store, and mix your own.

- When mixing paint with water, add a small amount of detergent. If your child gets paint on her clothes, it will wash right out.

Artist in Residence

Let a toddler color with crayons right on the highchair tray. Spray the tray with a laundry prewash product, and wash the tray in the sink. It should clean up easily. Or use WD-40.

Dishes for Paint and Water

- Use foam trays from supermarkets for artists' palettes. (You can also use them to make airplanes that really fly!)

- Mix colors only in the amounts needed in small jars or foam plastic egg cartons.

- Use the compartments of a molded, plastic ice cube tray for different colors.

- A plastic plate with dividers makes a good artist's palette for primary colors and water. A molded, plastic ice cube tray works well, too.

- Insert water or paint containers into holes you've cut in a rectangular sponge, to prevent tip-overs and to soak up overflow.

- Use an ashtray with cigarette rests and double-suction disks underneath as a water dish. It provides a place to rest a brush.

Personalized Hand Painting

- Make personalized handprint T-shirts as gifts or for kids to wear themselves. As a gift, have everyone in the family press their hand onto fabric paint spread over a paper plate. Then have them press their handprint onto a white T-shirt. Write each family member's name next to the handprint. Use a different color for each hand. Let children create their own personalized T-shirts using only their handprints in different colors on the front and back of the shirt.

- Make unique holiday cards using finger-painted handprints on white paper. To make a flower, add a stem and leaves. For a turkey, add an eye and legs.

- Let your kids paint on the bathtub with water-based finger paints. Afterward, just rinse the kids and the tub with water.

Brushes

- Let beginners paint with pastry brushes. (They pick up a lot of paint.) Or let them use cotton swabs or pipe cleaners with ends twisted into loops for painting that doesn't require fine line work. Even cut-up sponges do the job.

- Get brushes for toddlers at the hardware store. Brushes used for painting trim are wide enough and short-handled enough for them. Disposable sponge brushes are also good.

- Fill an empty, clean, roll-on deodorant bottle with paint, and let your kids roll paint on.

Recycling Crayons

There are several new crayon products on the market today that are worth investigating. Visit www.crayola.com. Still, these tips on recycling crayons will come in handy.

- Avoid arguments over using basic crayon colors by buying a big box with lots of pretty shades and two extra boxes of the eight basic colors.

- Sharpen crayons by dipping them in hot water and rolling them to a point between your thumb and forefinger. Or use a vegetable peeler.

- Make "double color" crayons by removing the paper from two crayons the same length, melting one side of each over a flame, and letting them dry together. Or bind them (or more) together with a rubber band.

- Melt old crayon pieces (with paper removed) in empty juice cans set in hot water over medium heat or in baby food jars in an electric skillet filled with water. Pour the wax into candy molds or the cups of an old muffin tin, cool, and remove. Seasonal molds work great!

- Reinforce crayons or chalk by wrapping transparent tape around them.

Cleaning Up after Crayons

Remove crayon from a chalkboard using WD-40. On wallpaper use a piece of white bread. On other places try to soften it first with a hair dryer set on warm/hot, then wipe off with a tissue. Or cover the area with brown paper and run a warm iron over it.

Glue

- Use liquid starch as glue for kids. It works well on tissue paper collages, cutouts, overlays, or assembly work, and it dries overnight.

- Use up old clear nail polish as glue. The little brush is a good size for a child. Refill the empty bottle with regular glue.

- Use a clean plastic mustard container as a glue applicator.

- Put glue in one section of a foam egg carton, and put small items to be glued (macaroni, beans, rice, or whatever) in other sections.

- Keep paste fresh and smooth by adding a few drops of water before closing the jar.

- Lubricate the cap grooves of glue and paste containers with petroleum jelly for easy opening and closing.

- Experiment with the colored glues available.

Storing Materials

- Convert an inexpensive cardboard shoe organizer into an art center for the floor or dresser top.

- Install a cafe curtain rod as a dispenser for a big roll of shelf paper for children's drawing and painting activities. Hang up a pair of blunt-nosed scissors nearby so your children can help themselves.

- Use a kitchen cutlery tray to store art supplies and keep them separated.

- Poke holes in a block of Styrofoam with one colored marker, and stand markers up in the block to keep them together and visible for color selection.

- Clean out an empty bleach bottle, cut away a section, leave the handle, and you have an excellent tote for materials.

Preserving Drawings

- Preserve a crayon drawing by putting it face-up on the ironing board (with newspapers underneath to protect the pad) and laying a piece of cotton sheeting over it. Iron the fabric firmly at a low-to-medium setting until the drawing has been transferred to the cloth. Let it cool before moving it.

- Spray drawings with hair spray to preserve the paper and keep the colors from rubbing off.

- Soak special drawings in a solution that will give them "an estimated life of two hundred years" (so it's been claimed). Dissolve a milk of magnesia tablet in a quart of club soda, and let it sit overnight. Soak the paper in the solution for an hour, drain, and pat dry. Weight the corners down while drying. Move it carefully.

Your Artist on Display

Save artwork *you* like, let your kids keep the things *they* like, and encourage throwing away pieces no one especially likes. You'll cut down on the quantity of "keepers," and you'll help your children be more critical of their work. Your praise will be more believable, too.

- Reduce the clutter on the refrigerator by having each child choose a favorite picture to be framed in clear plastic. Date, sign, and display in the hallway.

- Decorate the inside of kitchen cabinet doors with your children's art.

- Use a big piece of cardboard as a bulletin board to hang paintings on when the refrigerator door is full.

- Attach drawings to painted surfaces with a dab of toothpaste on each corner.

- Show your appreciation of your child's artwork by hanging a piece in the living room in a frame with an easily removable back. Change the artwork frequently.

- Use excess art to brighten walls in the garage.

- Display artwork on a folding clothes-drying rack. Attach drawings with clip clothespins.

- Save boxes that have a frame design (such as those from curtains) to hold and display children's art or keepsakes.

- Make place mats of drawings or paintings by sealing them between two layers of clear Contact paper. Or insert drawings in plastic folders for changeable place mats.

- Display drawings under a clear plastic tablecloth or a sheet of clear vinyl. If you have a glass-covered table, slide artwork between the glass and the tabletop.

- Let your kids paste their drawings on formula cans, coffee cans, potato chip cans, or other cans with plastic lids. They make great gift containers and are reusable as containers for art supplies and other small objects.

- Punch holes in drawings and save them in loose-leaf notebooks. Or let your kids save the drawings they want by clipping them together with giant, colored plastic clips.

Pass-Along Art

- Let your child write notes to grandparents on the backs of drawings, thereby saving paper as well as getting the artwork out into the world where it will be appreciated.

- Let your child make gift-wrap by decorating white shelf paper with crayons or paints.

- Donate stacks of your children's artwork to a local nursing home. Let your toddler hand them out, and everyone will have a good time.

Save Art without Saving Art

- Take photos of your child standing by a display of his work posted on the refrigerator or someplace else. Later you can all look back and see the fine things created back then.

- Videotape your kids with their artwork so you won't have to store the stuff forever.

- Save drawer space by scanning the artwork to create digital files that can be sent by computer to interested relatives.

Save on Coloring Books

Make black-and-white photocopies of your child's favorite cartoon or movie characters. They're perfect for coloring.

Encouraging Reading

- Attach colored stickers to sets of book or tapes so your child can match them correctly.

- Buy a special book for each child for each holiday occasion, as a family tradition.

- Encourage the learning of shapes and letters by using small paper plates as flash cards.

- Keep your active child involved while you read aloud by letting her draw or paint. Or ask your child to bring a favorite stuffed animal along to "listen" to the story.

- Make audio recordings of your child's favorite stories to listen to when she's too tired to read. A tired child might like to listen to the tapes and follow along in the book. Remember to say "Beep" or ring a bell when you turn each page, just like the commercial book-and-tapes do!

- Reinforce nonboard books by covering the pages with transparent tape or Contact paper. It makes them unrippable as well as washable.

- Stock up on bargain-priced books at your local thrift shop or secondhand book store. Pass along or donate books your child is no longer interested in.

- Schedule a daily reading time during or after a meal, before a nap, at bedtime, and so on. Make it relaxed and fun—not a chore.

- Reward older children with extra reading time alone in bed for a few minutes after the usual lights-out time.

Electronic Learning and Entertainment

From TV to videos to computer games, electronics are the future. Our kids need to know how the technology of their generation works, but not at the expense of letting them become addicted to media that don't let them experience the rest of the world. It's good to set guidelines while your children are still preschoolers.

- Establish rules regarding time use, and enforce them consistently.

- Invest in videos you think are worthwhile rather than having your kids watch whatever is on TV.

- Trade "other time" (such as playing outdoors) against TV time or computer game time.

- Keep the TV remote or joystick out of reach rather than having it sit in front of the item it goes with.

Computer Savvy

Computers have become the learning tool of record. They've replaced flash cards for learning numbers and letters. They've also created new opportunities for artistic expression and reading practice.

- Place computer and/or game equipment in family areas so their use is visible to you.

- Don't pressure a preschooler if the mouse is hard to use. Coordination is not a sign of intelligence. Some kids pick it up quicker than others.

- Slow down the mouse speed for a young child. Go to the control panel and set the mouse speed on the slow setting.

- Invest in a smaller size mouse for a preschooler. You can always use it later to work with a laptop.

- Bookmark your kids' favorite Internet sites so they can access them easily.

- Don't assume software is good just because it's free. Any software, even stuff you buy, needs to be appropriate to your child's skill level. The Internet is a good place to research software. Check out sites such as www.edutainingKids.com.

- Install Internet filters early on so they're a given instead of something you add later that piques your child's interest.

Preparing for School

- Check out books from the library that tell stories about the first day of school.

- Visit the school and let your child play on the playground equipment.

- Talk a lot about what school will be like, but be careful not to promise anything you're not sure will happen. Listen carefully to your child to discover fears and worries that may be lurking. Try to put yourself in your child's place. Some fears may seem silly to you, buy they're very real to your child.

- Help your child practice reciting his full name, address, and phone number. Setting it to music can make it easier to remember.

- Try role-playing. Let your child play both pupil and teacher.

- During the week before school, see if you can take a walking tour of the school with your child. Ask to meet your child's teacher during the visit. You might even want to photograph the classroom, cafeteria, and other important rooms so your child can be familiar with the school on the first day of class. Go to an open house or "get acquainted day" if your school has one.

- Make sure your child has seen and used public restrooms so as not to be intimidated by school bathrooms. Visit the ones at school, and make sure your child knows how to ask to go to the bathroom.

- Draw a big map including the home-to-school route and major landmarks. Let your child play with it using small cars or dolls.

- Walk to the bus stop (or the school itself) with your child before school starts. Go over any special arrangements for returning home, so your child truly understands the new routine. If your town has neighborhood safety programs, point out the "safe houses" to your child.

- Find out if there's a child in your neighborhood who will be walking the same route as your child, especially if you're new to the neighborhood. Introduce the children and allow them to get to know each other before the school year begins.

- Make sure your child has a familiar friend on the first day of school, if possible.

- Entering a classroom alone can be hard for a child. Try to arrange having your child arrive with a classmate.

- Give your child two gifts to help with scheduling: an alarm clock or clock radio (start setting it for bedtime and wake-up time) and a calendar to mark special days.

Organize for the Morning

- Establish the school-night bedtime before school starts, and stick to it. Get up early yourself and get things going on school days.

- Start selecting and laying out the next day's clothes the night before, including shoes and socks. Or have school outfits coordinated and hung in the closet. Give your child a choice of two outfits each day.

- Set the breakfast table before going to bed.

- Periodically check that all clocks in the house show the same time.

- Give your child incentives to keep moving (no breakfast until dressed, no TV until breakfast is eaten, and so on).

Learning Left from Right

Have your child form the letter *L* by holding up her left hand with fingers together and thumb stuck straight out. If your child is right-handed, she "writes with the right."

Off-to-School Routines

- Set a timer to help your child know when it's time to gather belongings and get ready to leave for school.

- Attach name tags to clothing that will be removed at school (sweaters, jackets, and so on).

- Tape milk money to the inside of your child's lunch bag or box so he can find it easily. Plastic sandwich bags work well to hold coins.

- Teach your child never to walk in front of the school bus until he sees the driver's eyes. This ensures that the driver sees your child, too!

- Supply your child with an empty paper towel tube for carrying important papers to and from school. In rainy weather, the tube can be slipped into a plastic bag for extra protection.

- Get your child a regular school bag or small backpack. (Either one is very grown-up.) A backpack won't wear out from being dragged on the ground, as a bag will.

- Keep large pins handy to pin notes-to-the-teacher on your child's clothing.

- Have the parent who works outside the home drop off the child the first few days. The child will be accustomed to saying good-bye to that parent, and it won't be so hard.

- Make sure your child understands that no one but a parent (or another designated person) can pick him up from school without written permission. Some families opt for a family password.

- Don't forget to ask your child each day about school activities. Listen very carefully to the answers in order to head off any problems. (Some children will share more than others.) Don't give your child the third degree! You may find that the best time to ask about the day's events is at night when you're tucking your child into bed.

Assuming you've now made it through *(and enjoyed)* your child's first five years, you now have the golden years (ages six to twelve) to look forward to. These are the years when children are still young enough to adore their parents, yet old enough to release them from the tremendous job of caring for small children. Enjoy these years, for beyond them is *adolescence!*

Index